Productivity and the Bonus Culture

Productivity and the Bonus Culture

Andrew Smithers

OXFORD
UNIVERSITY PRESS

OXFORD

UNIVERSITY PRESS

Great Clarendon Street, Oxford, OX2 6DP,
United Kingdom

Oxford University Press is a department of the University of Oxford.
It furthers the University's objective of excellence in research, scholarship,
and education by publishing worldwide. Oxford is a registered trade mark of
Oxford University Press in the UK and in certain other countries

First Edition published in 2019

Impression: 1

Published in the United States of America by Oxford University Press
198 Madison Avenue, New York, NY 10016, United States of America

British Library Cataloguing in Publication Data
Data available

Library of Congress Control Number: 2018955388

ISBN 978–0–19–883611–7

Printed and bound by
CPI Group (UK) Ltd, Croydon, CR0 4YY

To Vanessa Brown with abundant thanks.

Foreword by Martin Weale

This book presents a challenge to conventional economists like myself. There are two key strands to its argument—first that bonus arrangements, which I see as a form of profit sharing, have a large depressing effect on investment, and secondly that investment is the major determinant of growth in productivity, at least in the short-term—or at least that it is more important than conventional growth accounting implies.

It has been known for a long time that profit sharing is likely to lead to capital starvation. The explanation is very simple and is nothing to do with the widespread belief that businesses face a simple short-term budget constraint so that each pound paid out in bonuses is one pound less available for investment. Suppose that the required return on capital is five per cent per annum. If half of profits are paid out in bonuses or other forms of profit sharing, then any marginal unit of capital requires a return of ten per cent so that the people who supply the capital can earn the market return of five per cent. The outcome of this is that profit-sharing firms are likely to use less capital, so that the capital that they do have has a higher marginal product. Of course creditors are entitled to their interest before any profit-sharing takes place. As a result profit-sharing makes debt finance appear cheap relative to equity finance, and one would expect profit-sharing enterprises to be more highly geared than are conventional businesses. How far this effect was behind the increased gearing of the banking system in the period up to the financial crisis is unclear but it is hard to believe it was not material. Since then, of course, policy has focused on imposing capital ratios on the banks rather than addressing the incentives that lead to high gearing. That is perhaps reasonable because one could not be confident that, say, an income tax surcharge on profit shares would itself be enough to address the issue. After all, banking crises pre-dated profit sharing.

This argument, however, applies only to businesses which distribute a material proportion of their profits as a profit share paid to labour. A rather different and more subtle argument is needed to claim much more generally that bonuses depress investment. That in the book takes the following lines. Shareholders do not, at the margin, like the uncertainty associated with investment, so a large company investment programme is likely to depress the share price.

If decision-makers' remuneration is linked to share prices, and they do not expect to be in post for long enough for the benefits of a big investment programme to appear, then they will, with bonuses linked to company performance, be reluctant to embark on investment. Separately they might try to raise the share price through techniques such as share buy-backs and other capital reductions. If markets were efficient these two might be unrelated to each other, but buy-backs may be hard to deliver if, as a result of new investment, the need for capital is increasing. Of course the Modigliani–Miller theorem says that investors can unwind or wind up any gearing that a business does, and look through the financial structure of a business. But that may not be the case if shareholders are myopic.

Andrew Smithers augments these arguments with the point that increased investment often depresses profits in the short-term because its immediate effect is to increase depreciation; the benefits of extra investment may emerge only later. If investors are unable to distinguish the effects of investment from the effects of worsening market conditions or poor management, then this may influence share prices, with the consequence that managers' bonus payments are affected. Of course businesses should be able to explain the connection between investment and depreciation allowances, but market participants may not want to listen and markets may be unforgiving. Such an effect may be augmented if managers expect to be able to obtain a higher return on capital than is realistic. Both of these effects raise the hurdle rate on investment.

If bonus arrangements have the effect of depressing business investment, one might think that would leave a range of unexploited opportunities available to new entrants who do not get distracted by bonus arrangements. But there may well be barriers to entry which stop this happening.

It is generally recognized now that the slow-down in productivity growth globally came before the financial crisis. For example, in the US productivity growth seems to have been slower from 2005 onwards. What is less clear, however, is whether weak investment was a consequence or a cause of slower labour-saving technical progress. This book suggests that both factors are present. Technical progress has indeed been slower, depressing investment, but at the same time changes in non-technical variables, and notably the rise in the hurdle rate, have held back investment.

Andrew Smithers rejects the conventional growth accounting framework as a means of determining the contribution of investment to economic growth, on the grounds that the technology of the time is embedded in investment as it takes place. Thus technical progress and investment are intertwined in a way which growth accounting does not generally recognize. In this case very stringent assumptions are needed for the growth accounting framework to function—most notably that the labour/capital ratio has to be as flexible on old capital as it is before capital is installed. Such a 'putty-putty' proposition seems most unlikely to be true.

Having explained the limitations of growth accounting, Andrew Smithers then explains cogently the weaknesses of some of the other arguments that have been put forward to explain slow growth since the crisis. These arguments typically rely on the assumption that more demand would have delivered faster growth. The nub of the critique is that, with unemployment at low levels in the United States, Germany, and the United Kingdom, it is hard to argue that the problem lies on the demand side in these economies although it may do elsewhere in Europe. This argument of course applies to a range of possible sources of weak demand—debt reduction, budgetary stringency and deflation. He reminds us that US GDP grew more than threefold during the deflation of the late nineteenth century.

Finally we are presented with proposals intended to undo the effects of the bonus culture. If bonuses were treated like dividends as a payment out of post-tax profits, they would become more expensive and therefore less popular, or at least smaller. Possibly bonuses might require approval from competition authorities, or might be conditional on firms' achieving productivity targets. One obstacle the latter face is that, in my experience, some business people confuse profitability with productivity. At least that was what researchers at the National Institute found when trying to compare productivity in businesses in the UK with those in the Netherlands and Germany.

We can, however, go beyond the book to offer some indication of the near-term effect of more investment. If the capital stock consisted of equal amounts of capital representing all the economically viable vintages, then the share of income accruing to capital on new capital would be twice that of the average. The current gross social rate of return on capital in the United Kingdom, calculated as gross operating surplus divided by the purchase cost revalued to current prices, of the industrial capital stock, is about 12.5% per annum. In the absence of vintage effects, an increase of net investment of 1% of GDP would increase output by 0.125%. But if the immediate return on new capital is twice that of the average, then the immediate effect of increasing investment by 1% of GDP would be to raise output by about 0.25% of GDP. The faster growth would, however, be a temporary phenomenon as the economy adjusted to a higher capital/output ratio. Without any change in technical progress the end result of a higher investment ratio would be more income and a younger capital stock. But productivity growth would still eventually be constrained by technical progress.

Professor Martin Weale, CBE

Acknowledgements

This book owes a great debt to three groups of people: economists with whom I have discussed the ideas on which it is based, friends who are not economists but who have kindly read the book and provided suggestions and encouragement, and Vanessa Brown, my PA, to whom it is dedicated.

Among economists my special thanks goes to Martin Weale with whom I have discussed in detail and over many hours my TFP model. I owe to Stephen Wright our joint destruction of the EMH and the evidence that the cost of capital is not, as it is usually presented, a determinant of the level of investment. I worked with James Mitchell on depreciation, which is central to TFP models and which is frequently confused with the costs of maintenance. In the text I acknowledge my debt to Martin Wolf for driving me to produce my TFP model, but I owe him much more through his patience in numerous and detailed discussions of other important issues. Charles Goodhart has been a steady supporter of my central thesis and drawn my attention to many papers which appertain to it and which I might otherwise have missed. I should, however, add that he disclaims any profound knowledge of the TFP debate. I also thank Robin Harding for drawing my attention to one of the key papers which I quote. Nick Oulton has been kind enough to discuss my ideas despite having produced a paper which follows the alternative approach to TFP.

Jonathan Steinberg and Simon May are the friends who were sufficiently interested to read the book in an early draft, and I am most grateful for their kindness and encouragement.

Vanessa has worked with me for eighteen years. She has proofread nearly everything I have written, corrected errors, and drawn attention to my failures to communicate the ideas with sufficient clarity. She has also been a stalwart supporter and has dealt with all those whose help has been needed for this book with a tact and charm of which I have been the underserved beneficiary.

The philosophic basis of my approach to economics owes an enormous debt to Karl Popper; my interest in the subject is the result of having had the good fortune to have been taught by Brian Reddaway as an undergraduate.

I should add that in acknowledging my thanks I am not claiming that those mentioned will necessarily agree with all my conclusions.

Contents

Contents

List of Figures

List of Tables

1

The Legacy of the Financial Crisis

A decade has passed since the financial crisis, but its impact is still with us. The developed world has since grown slowly and many economists and financial journalists believe that the two are connected. This belief is both very important and totally wrong. It also provides an example of how damaging misguided views can be. As I shall show, the financial crisis had almost nothing to do with the slow growth that has since occurred in the UK and the US, but the connection has become a deeply embedded myth. The near-stagnation of the UK and US economies after the financial crisis is the result of changes that pre-date it by thirty years or more. Policy must change if we are to avoid being caught in a depressing and politically dangerous torpor. But the belief that the crisis was the cause of our weak growth has inhibited the introduction of the policy changes needed. To restore an acceptable rate of growth we require new policies. A lively public debate, leading to widespread understanding of the need for them, is an essential step towards their introduction. The myth that low growth and poor productivity are the result of the financial crisis has become a major problem because it has largely prevented this necessary debate from taking place. In this sense and in this sense only, the financial crisis has been the cause of the subsequent slow growth and it is likely to continue to impede progress until this misconception ends.

Because any analysis of economic issues needs debate and must stand up to it, this book is intended to be read by economists. Because a widespread discussion and understanding of our problems is an essential step towards solving them, this book is also addressed to the wider and less specialized audience of those who are concerned with the economic and political future of the two major Anglophone democracies. In order to appeal to both audiences I have tried to avoid in the text a technical presentation of the underlying economics, but I have also sought to show that my case is strongly (I hope overwhelmingly) supported by the data. The evidence of the data is by itself sufficient justification for the policies that I recommend. But we reasonably seek to comprehend how things work. Without such understanding, policy would appear to be based on the hidden working of some black box. This would not only be intellectually unsatisfactory, it would hold back acceptance of the case I present. I have therefore set out, as far as I can in non-technical terms, a model which is not only consistent with the data but also explains the essential link between productivity and the capital stock, which is the basis upon which my policy recommendations rest. I hope that this will satisfy both the non-specialist reader and economists. With the broader audience in mind I have sought to restrict technical points to the footnotes and appendices.

The model shows that growth is not solely dependent on the speed of technological change. This is fortunate because we seem to be unable through policy changes to have any impact on that rate. I show that growth also depends on how much investment can be financed at any given level of technology and that policy can affect the level of investment and thus growth. We do not have to accept slow growth as a necessary condition of our future. This is of vital importance as slow growth in output can easily become stagnation of living standards, which in recent years most voters in the developed world have experienced. Unless we introduce new policies this will continue so that, when the next recession hits, not only will living standards fall but they will have fallen over several years. Voters are already showing dissatisfaction with the way economies are being run, and are right to do so. Unfortunately they often heed the views of politicians who, if elected, are likely to make matters worse rather than better, and whose attraction is frequently based on the claim that they are not actually politicians, or at least not cast in the old mould. But a change of leaders will not improve matters unless it leads to better policies; and the new populists, who lambast stagnation and promise recovery, produce no credible policies to support their pledges. Some blame foreigners and advocate protection, a course which would reduce the efficiency of capital and slow trend growth even more. Others promise a rise in living standards through the redistribution of incomes and generalized attacks on business. This does not address the fundamental problem, which is slow growth and is not, for the most part, due to increased inequality of incomes. In the UK for example inequality has fallen rather than risen since the financial crisis and, although this is not true for the US, the World Bank calculates that on a worldwide basis it is generally true.[1] As the debate over inequality is no less fierce in the UK than it is in the US, this suggests that the fundamental cause of discontent is the stagnation of incomes rather than their distribution. Successful attempts to reduce inequality are desirable, provided that they do not damage liberty or reduce welfare through their negative impact on growth, but populist policies tend to have just these damaging effects. We

---

[1] Donnan (2016).

require a major change in business behaviour leading to higher investment. Successful policies to achieve this may make the distribution of incomes more even, but policies which aim primarily at improving income equality will fail to halt the stagnation of living standards. They will probably accentuate rather than reverse the weakness of investment, which is the key problem. Populist policies tend either to encourage consumption at the expense of investment or to boost demand beyond the capacity of the economy to meet it, with the result that output has to be sharply curtailed to prevent rising inflation.

Conventional wisdom condoned the policies which allowed 'the great' 2008 recession, and now fails to understand why growth has since been so poor. This has led to claims that we should not listen to experts. But we no more need amateur economists than amateur brain surgeons. The solution does not lie in abandoning reason but encouraging its use and thereby improving our understanding. In an educated democracy we are responsible for ensuring that conventional wisdom is not moribund but is, through public debate, exposed to serious ideas. If these are not only serious but sound, conventional wisdom should change. This book proposes the new policies which are needed to avoid stagnation and the political threat which continued stagnation entails. It is therefore an attempt to change current conventional wisdom. While I naturally hope that my ideas will stand up to the rigour of public debate, the first step is to have such a debate.

The financial crisis, and the great recession which followed, were the results of poor management, arising from the misplaced faith of central banks and governments in an inadequate model of the economy. This is widely, though not yet universally, accepted and there has been a shift from the pre-crisis complacency to the recognition of our errors in economic management. Alan Blinder, former vice chairman of the Federal Reserve, claimed at the height of the stock market boom of 1999 that 'For the US economy to go into significant recession, never mind a depression, important policy makers will have to take leave of their senses.'[2] This is in sharp contrast to the post-crisis views of Mervyn King, former Governor of the Bank of England, who recently wrote that 'The crisis was a failure of the system, and the ideas that underpinned it . . . There was a general misunderstanding of how the world economy worked.'[3] It is now largely agreed that the model of the economy on which pre-crisis policy was based was unsound. Among its errors were the views that financial markets could not become overpriced and that debt could not rise to excessive levels. Experience, which persuades more readily than argument, has exposed these follies. This recognition is a great advance and much energy is now being expended on how to avoid another financial

---

[2] Snowdon (2001).   [3] King (2016).

crisis. Unfortunately these past errors are not the only weaknesses of current economic policy and the way it is debated. Erroneous views, whose influence on policy threatens our future, are being widely promulgated. Even if we avoid another financial crisis or major recession, the policies of today's governments and central banks are unlikely to produce enough growth to sustain the support of electorates. Poor economic theory led to the financial crisis and poor theory is still with us. There is a general failure to recognize that the fundamental problem for the UK and the US is not that of inadequate demand, but a lack of potential supply due to insufficient investment.

Even before the financial crisis, it was clear that the economic theory on which policy was based was unsound because it depended on the hypothesis of financial market efficiency, which was untestable and thus unscientific.[4] The financial crisis was not needed to show this: it simply forced home the point on an audience that had previously been unwilling to accept it. The adherence of policymakers to an inadequate model of the economy was a major cause of the crisis. It was the impact of the crisis which changed minds. We must hope and seek to ensure that we can emend the current faults of policy without the need for another crisis.

Until recently the numbers of those able and willing to work in the UK and the US had risen more rapidly than the total population. As a result, living standards rose faster than productivity. This situation has now reversed: living standards will now lag the rise in productivity. Unfortunately this change has been accompanied by a marked fall in the rate at which productivity has risen. An improvement in productivity is now needed to ensure that GDP per head does not fall. Even if growth is good enough to allow incomes per person to rise slowly, there will nonetheless be a fall in most people's living standards if the distribution of incomes becomes increasingly uneven. Even a rise in GDP per head will not prevent the majority of the population from experiencing a fall in their real income if a disproportionate part of the rise is captured by the rising prosperity of a minority.

Investment started to slow long before the financial crisis and is now too low to ensure that living standards do not decline. Those who blame weak growth on the financial crisis are thus forced to deny the connection between growth and investment. Those unaffected by this myth are right to think that such a relationship is sufficiently probable to warrant detailed consideration. That this is seldom done shows the remarkable power of myth. Among the key reasons why conventional wisdom is astray is the simple-minded assumption

---

[4] The original hypothesis, the random walk model, was testable but when tested was shown to be invalid. Reflecting their reluctance to discard the underlying assumption, its proponents modified the hypothesis by adding other assumptions including ones about investor preferences. This made the revised hypothesis untestable and the adherence of its proponents to it was thus unscientific.

that because weak growth followed the crisis it was caused by it. Logicians emphasize the folly of this view, which is known as 'post hoc ergo propter hoc' (after this because of this), and their cautions need emphasizing because today, as so often, they are being ignored.

It is widely but wrongly held that our weak growth is the result of the financial crisis. But neither the crisis nor the subsequent recession can be sensibly blamed for either the demographic change or poor productivity. I will show that these have been the twin and only causes of stagnation. The adverse change in demography resulted from the fall in the birth rate and poor productivity from the decline in growth of the capital stock, which dates from well before the crisis and resulted from the earlier fall in investment. The fundamental causes of the slow growth of the past decade in the UK and the US were thus the declines in the birth rate and investment, which both pre-date the crisis by many years.

Even if we could and wished to reverse the decline in the birth rate, it would take fifteen to twenty years before the problem posed by the past fall ceased to have an adverse impact. To halt the stagnation of living standards will thus be impossible if we cannot improve productivity. Happily this is possible, as we can increase the speed at which the net capital stock grows. To do this we need a major increase in the level of investment and I suggest how this can be done. Unfortunately discussion of this essential change in policy is being held back by an instinctive acceptance of the post hoc fallacy, reinforced by the current weaknesses and biases in the way the economic debate is conducted, which often assume that growth is solely dependent on changes in technology whose speed we seem unable to improve.

One of the weirdest features of current conventional wisdom is the widespread belief that poor productivity is inexplicable. There are many competing models of the economy and most of these cannot account for the decline in productivity. But this is evidence not that the decline in productivity is inexplicable, but that these models should be discarded in favour of those which are supported by the evidence and provide a satisfactory explanation of our dilemma. I shall show that the decline in productivity is explained by the fall in investment and that the hypothesis on which this theory rests is testable and proves to be robust when tested. It should therefore be held in preference to models which claim that poor productivity is inexplicable and which are not, as far as I can find, based on any testable and robust hypothesis.[5] The US data show that growth of output has a stable relationship with the

---

[5] If these 'inexplicable' productivity models are not based on testable and robust hypotheses they fall, like the EMH, on the wrong side of Karl Popper's demarcation between science and non-science and are another example of economics being a science which is often pursued unscientifically (Popper 1959).

growth in the value of the net capital stock. As this varies with the past level of tangible investment, its decline provides a clear and obvious cause for the weakness in productivity and the data show that its origins date from well before the financial crisis. It should not be a cause for surprise that low investment has damaged productivity, but apparently it is. An example of the unwillingness to accept this likely connection is to be found in the leading article in the *Financial Times* of 30 May 2016, which claimed that productivity is 'the puzzle that baffles the world's economies' and, together with another article published the same day, ignored the probable connection between investment and productivity. The failure to admit the likelihood of the connection has been very damaging, as it deflects attention from why investment is so low. It has also influenced official forecasts, which have been habitually over-optimistic, being based on the assumption that productivity is about to bounce back.

Successful economic policy requires that we achieve four targets:

   (i) we must avoid another financial crisis;

  (ii) we must avoid a bad recession induced by inadequate demand;[6]

 (iii) we must avoid entering a sustained period in which the standard of living falls;

 (iv) we must avoid excessive inflation and a rise in inflationary expectations.

Until recently only the first and second of these four objectives have received any serious attention in the financial press or from the majority of policymakers. They are all, however, important, and if we concentrate on only half our problems it is probable that we will fail to deal with the others. The failure to give sufficient attention to the decline in our capacity to grow is largely due to the myth that the slow growth of the UK and US economies over the past eight years is due to the financial crisis. This has, in an incoherent but nonetheless effective way, led to the mistaken belief that our key problem is how to stimulate demand, not how to improve our long-term capacity for growth. We are suffering from a similar naivety to that which was shown in the UK's national plan of 1964, which failed because it 'focused on policies to boost the demand for goods and services rather than on the ability of the economy to produce them'.[7] Though it has taken a long time, there are at last signs that poor productivity is receiving attention, but there is still a reluctance to accept its connection with low investment, for which I will show there is overwhelming evidence.

---

[6] Some would claim that we should aim to avoid even mild recessions. There is, however, a strong case that mild recessions are necessary to avoid big ones.
[7] King (2016).

Academic economists have, to some extent justly, been accused of physics envy. This has led them to search for models of the economy which can be applied universally, like those of physics, and can be set out with mathematical elegance. This bias has encouraged the unscientific approach in which faith is put in models which simply don't work. An example, which was the fundamental cause of the financial crisis, is that faith was placed on the assumption that financial markets price assets efficiently. Misplaced confidence in this Efficient Market Hypothesis ('EMH') is largely to blame for the refusal of central bankers to recognize the risks posed in the run-up to the financial crisis by overpriced assets.[8] We have similar problems today with regard to investment. It is often assumed that capital spending rises and falls in response to the returns expected on new investments and the interest rates which are assumed to determine the cost of the capital needed to finance them. Since current returns on corporate investment are high, and recent experience largely determines current expectations, we should if this view were correct now be witnessing a satisfactory level of investment in response to the fall in interest rates to near zero. As we haven't, some economists have argued that we need higher inflation so that real interest rates, which are nominal ones minus inflation, can become significantly negative. The hypothesis on which this theory depends is that investment responds to real interest rates and not just to nominal ones. This hypothesis is testable and has failed when tested.[9] Nonetheless some economists continue to adhere to it and persist in maintaining the view that investment responds to real rather than nominal interest rates. This is not the only fault of this model, and adherence to it is, like the widespread pre-crisis faith in the EMH, an example of economics being pursued unscientifically. The prominent physicists David Deutsch and Artur Ekert have claimed that physicists are culpable of much bad science.[10] I am sadly confident that this criticism is as at least equally valid in economics. Fortunately there is growing dissatisfaction with many previously accepted views and I shall be quoting from Robert Gordon, Jean Tirole, and others whose work is helping to point out the errors of conventional wisdom.

Once the debate stops being inhibited by the post hoc myth, it should move to a discussion of why investment has remained so depressed despite low interest rates. Although the assumption that investment responds to real interest rates is often held despite its failure to stand up to testing, this objection cannot be held against nominal interest rates.[11] The failure of investment to respond satisfactorily to low interest rates is therefore a challenge to both

---

[8] For my detailed exposition of this point see Smithers (2009).
[9] Fair (2015). For details see Appendix 1.   [10] Deutsch and Ekert (2012).
[11] See Appendix 1.

theory and policy. In policy terms we need to find another way to stimulate investment and from the viewpoint of theory we need an explanation of why investment remains depressed despite the combination of near-zero interest rates and high returns on corporate equity. Until 2000 business investment and returns were strongly related. We therefore need to explain why things have changed rather than continue to ignore the question. That such a change has occurred, and how to undo the damage, is the central thesis of this book. There has been a major change in the incentives of senior management through the way and amount they are paid. Incentives determine behaviour, so we should not be surprised that behaviour changes when incentives change. I shall argue that the pay packages for management are formed today in a way that discourages investment. I shall also show that the apparent change in US corporate behaviour, in which investment ceased to respond to returns on equity or reductions in corporation tax, followed the change in the way managements are paid. The obvious conclusion is that we should change policy to reverse this adverse development. This runs up against a bias among economists in favour of explanations which rely on universal models. The change in management incentives applies to the UK and the US, and is far from being a worldwide phenomenon. It affects quoted much more than unquoted companies and in Europe, particularly in Germany, quoted companies constitute a much smaller proportion of business output than they do in the Anglophone economies. This is also true (though to a lesser extent) in Japan—where however there is also a very different business culture and management incentives. The slow recovery of the Eurozone has reflected weak demand rather than low investment. The change in the way management is paid in Anglophone economies, which is a completely new phenomenon, has set off a change in the way these economies work, so that a model which might have provided a satisfactory explanation of their past behaviour is no longer valid for today. A satisfactory model of the behaviour of the world economy after the financial crisis is therefore specific in terms of geography and time, and is thus unsettling for those who look for universal models.

The search for models which can be applied generally has often proved fruitful. An outstanding example is John Maynard Keynes's explanation of how divergent intentions to save and to invest can lead to inadequate demand and unemployment. This approach has therefore been extremely valuable in periods (such as the slump) when problems of insufficient demand have been worldwide. At times, however, it is essential to concentrate on the differences between economies. There have been periods when different economies suffered from their own very particular ills. In the 1920s the UK suffered from recession, unemployment and deflation, while the US had strong growth, full employment and rising prices, and Germany had hyperinflation. The UK's unemployment averaged 8.2 per cent from 1922 to 1926 and prices fell at 5.6 per cent per annum. In the US unemployment averaged 3.8 per cent and prices rose at 3.4 per cent per annum. Today there is a wide disparity between the Anglophone economies, which combine full employment with low growth, and the Eurozone which has had both low growth and widespread unemployment. In today's policy debate these differences are often ignored. There have been frequent calls for more fiscal stimulus on the grounds that there is spare capacity in the world as a whole. As unemployment remains high in the Eurozone its growth would accelerate in response to fiscal stimulus, but none is needed in the UK or the US where recent changes are already excessive.

The major cause of weak investment and thus productivity in the UK and the US has been the change in the way senior management is paid. The bonus culture of today provides a strong disincentive to invest, and the failure to give due regard to the problem and the causes of weak investment and productivity has meant that it has been difficult to get this issue seriously discussed in the financial press. On most occasions when the pay of corporate managers is raised it is wrongly perceived as a problem for shareholders. Investment has been depressed by the perverse incentives of the bonus culture, which has had a bad impact on the economy similar to that of a rise in monopoly power. A rise in monopoly is bad for the economy but not for shareholders. To end the perverse incentives is thus a job for governments, not shareholders, and I suggest how it should be tackled. My aims are to get attention to the problem of low investment, to induce an understanding of its cause and show that it can be tackled.

We need a change either in the incentives of the bonus culture or in their impact on the economy. I suggest ways in which each might be achieved. I think that it is likely, for example, that business investment could be increased through changes in the allowances for depreciation, as even with unchanged incentives the impact of investment on bonuses would change. Increasing public sector investment is another possible way of raising our potential for growth. Underinvestment in infrastructure, which is often publicly financed, may not simply be a route to higher growth but an essential ingredient. There is, however, much misunderstanding about this, as it seems to be widely believed that more public investment does not involve cuts in other expenditure or increased taxes to pay for it. This is only true if there are unused resources of labour and capital. Increased fiscal deficits would thus have been helpful in the Eurozone, but not in the UK and the US, which currently appear to have full employment. If a rise in investment can be successfully achieved in either the public or the private sector, then an equal rise in savings will be necessary to finance it. While a change in depreciation allowances should increase corporate savings as well as investment, some additional increase in national savings through a fall in the fiscal deficit is likely to be necessary in Anglophone economies, and this is likely to be politically unpopular. The economic consequences of higher investment are an improvement in our longer-term outlook combined with a shorter-term constraint on consumption, which is an example of Milton Friedman's well known dictum that in economics there are no free lunches.

Decisions are made by individuals not by abstractions called companies, which do not always behave in the interests of their owners. Those managers who determine the level of their companies' investment are mindful of their own interests. Economies do not therefore behave as if companies did not exist. There is a 'corporate veil' between the actions that their owners would take and those that are taken. While the existence and importance of the corporate veil is accepted in principle by most economists, it is often ignored in practice. It is common, for example, to encounter explanations for changes in the savings of the private sector which depend on the ageing of the population and thereby assume that companies will respond to the ageing of their shareholders rather than to the interests of their managements. The corporate sector makes a major contribution to total national savings and swings in the sector's savings have been large and have moved closely with fiscal deficits. As companies' savings have been so important and have often moved in a different way to those of the household sector, savings' models which assume that there is no corporate veil have not worked: these provide another example of the way that economics can be approached unscientifically. The corporate veil affects investment as well as savings, and the rise of the bonus culture has had the effect of thickening the veil, so that investment is depressed in the interests of management even when it would be highly profitable. This does not, however, give rise to conflict between management and shareholders, as the latter are concerned with their wealth rather than with the underlying value of the companies in which they invest.

It is difficult for those who studied economics at university, but have left academia, to keep up to date. On occasion views which used to be held by economists, but which have largely been discarded, continue to be promulgated in the press, and are part of the barrage of misinformation to which we are subject. Another major source is the biased publications of investment bankers on which journalists heavily rely. This even affects the views of economists. Unless it relates to their specialist field, much of the information on which economists base their general views is drawn from the press and much of this is wrong. Misinformation thus has wide ramifications and it is not stifled unless those who have specialized knowledge know that it is being promulgated and take the trouble to correct it. One current and common form of misinformation is over corporate returns on equity. Their overstatement leads to excessive expectations about the returns that companies should require on their new investment and this provides support for corporate managements who wish, in their own interests but in opposition to those of the economy, to keep investment low. Misinformation probably makes a significant contribution to amplifying the damage done by the bonus culture. There are times when the old press adage of 'simplify and then exaggerate' has degenerated to 'misunderstand, misinform, and mislead'. It recalls the old joke 'He was dropped on his head when young and believes what he reads in the newspapers.' I recommend a way for us to reverse the incentives which currently inhibit investment. If implemented it would have the subsidiary benefit of improving the information we have about companies and thus, I hope, making it easier to correct some of the battery of misinformation from which we suffer.

The conditions in which additional demand is needed even in the UK and the US may return, and it can therefore be claimed that they are needed now because a return of these conditions is imminent. While a boost to demand may be required we should in general be sceptical of such claims. Economic forecasts are notoriously fallible, and those whose past judgements have proved misguided often prefer to claim that they were not wrong but simply premature, thereby ducking the need to recognize their mistakes. An unwillingness to admit past error is all too human, but it is aggravated by the excessive importance placed on economic forecasts. A correct view about the toss of one coin is not a sensible guide to the validity of any tossing theory that the forecaster may hold. Because forecasts are so unreliable, we must not use individual outturns as the sole criterion for assessing the validity of economic analyses and theories. An unfortunate effect of this excessive emphasis on forecasts has been a reluctance of those who called for more fiscal stimulus to accept why they were wrong. In general at least, the advocates of additional fiscal stimuli were wrong because this was unnecessary. Their error was not that the UK and the US grew faster than they anticipated but lay in assuming a much faster ability to grow than has proved to be the case. Excessive anxiety to avoid admitting error has led to unwillingness to accept the extent to which our ability to grow has slowed. This has led to over-optimistic estimates of trend growth rates and encourages resistance to tougher monetary policy.

The UK's vote to leave the European Union may reduce demand. If it does, this can easily be offset by more fiscal stimulus. A demand impact should not therefore pose a serious problem, unless the response is badly handled. A more serious problem lies in the damage that Brexit will do to the UK's supply capacity and thus its ability to grow over time. The problem of weak growth which was posed before has been made worse by the vote to leave and the need for policy measures to offset the threat to living standards has thus become even more urgent.

Since the end of World War II we have become used to a steady rise in living standards. We face the risk that this will now end. Individuals can respond bravely to poverty and badly to wealth, but the impact on whole countries of declining living standards has almost invariably been bad, with the rise in fascism and communism between the two world wars being an outstanding example. We have had one major policy failure and currently face major risks of two more. One is the risk of another financial crisis. The other is that growth will not be sufficient to sustain voters' faith in traditional parties. Those who leap to power when this occurs often espouse even worse policies, which lead not to recovery but to even greater failure. I am not forecasting that we will suffer from such a fall in living standards. But we do face a serious risk and we should alter policy to prevent it materializing. We need therefore to accept that we need more investment to boost productivity and that the current perverse incentives of the bonus culture must be changed to do this.

Individuals suffer when the skills they have acquired become useless. Such disruption is part of the price of growth, which has also mitigated its pain. We are today faced with disruption with little reward. This encourages policies to reduce disruption at the expense of even lower growth.

The failure of the Anglophone economies to grow has not only given rise to the danger of domestic policies which will make it worse, it has also damaged the standing of liberal democracies compared with the state sponsored capitalism of China and Russia.

2

What I Seek to Show

I propose that we change current economic policy. Without a major revision we face a high risk that living standards in the UK and the US will fall. The added risk is that this would encourage populist policies which would accelerate the decline.

(i) My first step is to compare growth rates before and after the financial crisis. I examine the contributions to the decline in growth made by changes in unemployment, willingness to work, hours worked, productivity, and the growth in the workforce. From this analysis I show that the decline in growth rates since the financial crisis has been solely due to changes in demography and productivity.

(ii) I then show that the adverse change in demography is the result of a change in birth rates and that the loss in productivity is due to the decline in tangible investment. Both these changes pre-date the financial crisis by many years, and cannot have been caused by it. Those who assume that the financial crisis caused the subsequent slowdown in growth have thus fallen into the trap of the 'post hoc fallacy'.

(iii) The decline in the birth rates, which started in the 1960s, has had a long-delayed impact on the subsequent growth in the populations of working age. In due course it will start to reduce the growth of the total populations. For some years ahead, however, the populations of working age will be growing more slowly than the populations as a whole: this depresses standards of living.

(iv) This adverse change in demography could be reversed by more immigration, but this is unlikely as popular opinion increasingly favours further restrictions. It could also be offset by raising retirement ages and by encouraging those who are retired to continue working. Such policies might make a useful contribution to mitigating the threat and should be encouraged.

(v) Before the crisis the workforce in both the UK and the US was growing faster than the population, so that living standards grew faster than productivity. They will now grow more slowly. An increase in productivity is thus needed to offset the negative impact of demography.

(vi) I show that productivity depends on the amount of capital equipment that is available for workers to use. US data show that the value of the net capital stock rises in line with output; consequently the rate at which productivity improves moves with changes in the growth of this measure of the net capital stock.

(vii) The evidence that productivity depends on the level of the net capital stock is sometimes resisted on the false assumption that it conflicts with the generally accepted description of the economy termed Total Factor Productivity (TFP). This quite reasonably holds that productivity depends not only on the level of investment but also on improvements in technology and workforce education. I show, however, that there is no conflict between the evidence that output depends on the level of the net capital stock and a valid model of TFP.

(viii) Tangible investment has embedded in it the technology of its time. Recently invested capital is more valuable than old because it is more productive. The current value of old capital and the rate at which it falls over time depends significantly on the growth of productivity and thus on the rate at which technology improves. The value of the net capital stock thus includes an adjustment for the rate of technological progress as well as the total amount of past investment.

(ix) TFP provides a convincing description of the various inputs that contribute to productivity. But descriptions are not models and before starting to write this book I was unable to find a valid model for TFP that explains changes in labour productivity. I have therefore since published a new model[1] whose validity is shown by being based on testable hypotheses which are robust when tested.[2]

(x) This TFP model provides support for the conclusion that public policy needs to change management incentives and for the hypothesis that labour productivity depends on the volume of the net tangible capital stock. Measured by volume rather than value,[3] the net tangible capital stock rises if investment in it is greater than the amount of capital scrapped. To increase the growth of the volume of the net capital stock we therefore need to increase the proportion of GDP invested in tangible capital.

---

[1] See Smithers (2017). I have since revised this model and hope to publish the revised version shortly. The description in this book reflects the revisions I have made to the earlier paper.

[2] Since my *World Economics* paper was published I have produced additional tests for my model which it passes successfully and the results of these are included in this book.

[3] See Chapter 8.

(xi) My model shows that growth is not solely dependent on the speed of change in technology, but can be enhanced by policy changes which lead to more investment.

(xii) In 2013 there was a major change, applied retrospectively, in the way GDP is calculated. The change increased both the measured value of GDP and the proportion invested, though of course the underlying reality was not affected. This change has been largely unnoticed and there has therefore been a failure to appreciate the extent to which tangible investment has fallen. Another underappreciated impact of this change is that the slowdown in the growth of the net capital stock, measured by volume, has been much faster than the fall in total investment including that made in intangibles.

(xiii) The level of investment is determined by the interaction between expected returns and the return required to justify investment. In addition to changes in technology both expected and required returns are dependent on a number of non-technology variables (NTVs), an important constituent of which is the return on equity that companies demand to justify investment, known as the hurdle rate. The data show that companies have a stable long-term hurdle rate measured in terms of the real return on corporate equity, but short-term changes in this rate can nonetheless be very important in determining the level of investment.

(xiv) There has been a major change in the incentives that influence the behaviour of senior management in the UK and the US. I explain why this has encouraged lower investment, higher profit margins, and increased volatility of the published profits of quoted companies compared with those in the national accounts. I show that each of these expected changes has occurred following the dramatic change in management incentives and is readily explained by them.

(xv) Before this change in the way companies behave, the level of investment moved up and down with returns on corporate equity and the effective rate of corporation tax. As current returns are likely to be a major determinant of expected ones, the data suggest that investment moved in line with anticipated returns. I show from US data that this theory was in line with the outturn until 2000, when there appears to have been a change in behaviour. There was a strong statistical relationship between returns on corporate equity and the effective rate of corporation tax compared with levels of investment up to 2000, but none thereafter.

(xvi) Although TFP has fallen over the past thirty years there is no evidence of any further recent deterioration. The weakness of investment points therefore to deterioration in NTV all of whose constituents except the hurdle rate have improved. There must therefore have been a large rise in the hurdle rate after 2000. This follows closely on the change in the way management is paid, and thus adds to the evidence that the consequent change in management behaviour has caused the weakness of investment.

(xvii) Unfortunately we do not have similar long-term data on returns on corporate equity and investment for the UK. But as the short-term data on investment show a similar pattern to the US, and there has been a similar change in the way management is paid in the UK, it is likely that the bonus culture has led to the fall in investment and thus productivity in both countries.

(xviii) There is therefore strong evidence that the poor growth in the volume of the net capital stock has been caused by the change in management incentives. As the slow growth of the capital stock has caused the weakness of productivity, either the perverse management incentives must be reversed or changes made in depreciation allowances so that current incentives encourage investment. Unless we make one or other of these changes we are unlikely to be able to achieve a satisfactory improvement in productivity.

(xix) The changes in management behaviour have been accompanied by an otherwise unexpected rise in corporate profit margins. These are also likely to widen if there is a fall in competition. A rise in profit margins, which can arise either from the change in incentives induced by the bonus culture or a decline in competition, is not contrary to the interests of shareholders: we cannot therefore expect shareholders to seek to increase competition or to challenge the bonus culture.

(xx) I discuss claims that a rise in business concentration explains the high level of profit margins and a low level of investment. Long-term data for testing the implied hypothesis are not available whereas those for management pay are. The bonus culture theory is thus based on a testable hypothesis and should be preferred to the business concentration theory, which is not. The volatility of published relative to national account profits and the relative decline in investment by large quoted companies are explained by the bonus culture but not by reduced competition. These provide additional evidence to support preference being given to the bonus culture explanation.

(xxi) Most of the public debate on management pay has centred on the response that shareholders should have to the rise in management pay. This has unfortunately deflected debate away from the damage being done to economic growth by the bonus culture. The bonus culture damages the economy rather than shareholders and its reform must therefore be a job for governments not shareholders.

(xxii) I suggest that these authorities have the power to approve incentive schemes provided they include productivity targets. Companies would not be forced to have their incentive schemes approved, but would be encouraged to do so by tax advantages.

(xxiii) An alternative would be to allow companies to depreciate for tax purposes 100 per cent of new investment in the first year. This would not change the incentive but it should change the response as increased investment would then become in the interests of management.

(xxiv) An increase in investment is a necessary condition for ending the threat to our living standards. I warn that this must be accompanied and paid for by a rise in national savings, which will probably require declines in fiscal deficits. Consumption needs to fall as a proportion of GDP if investment is to rise, and this will not be popular in the short-term.

3

Poor Productivity and Damaging Demography

Before the financial crisis, as Figure 1 shows, the growth rates of both the UK and the US were similar and, by both long-term and subsequent standards, unusually stable. This ended in 2008 with GDP peaking for the UK in Q1 2008 and for the US in Q4 2007. Had growth continued unabated at the rates achieved from Q1 1995 to Q4 2007, GDP would have been 20.2 per cent higher in the UK and 18.4 per cent in the US by Q4 2017.

The slow rate at which the economies grew after the crisis could have had two very different causes. It could have been a problem either of demand—which might have been insufficient to absorb the potential capacity of the two economies to provide goods and services—or of supply, in which case the growth of potential output must have slowed.

Table 1 shows, however, that unemployment has fallen since Q4 2007, so weak demand cannot have been to blame, and the decline in growth must have come from a slowdown in the economy's capacity to grow. Growth depends on the total number of hours that people work and their output per hour, which measures productivity. I shall therefore seek to identify the possible causes for changes in both hours worked and productivity and then, by measuring the impact that each change had on GDP, assess their relative importance. By doing this I shall show that the entire decline in potential growth in both the UK and the US was due to a combination of changes in the growth of the population of working age and in the output per hour of those employed.

If we compare the rate of change in the number of people employed from 1995 to 2007 with that since, we see that there has been a marked deceleration, which has been largely due to a slowdown in the growth of the population of working age. But such demographic effects are not the only way in which changes occur in the number of hours worked. There are variations in the willingness to work, the ability of the willing to find work and the number of hours each person

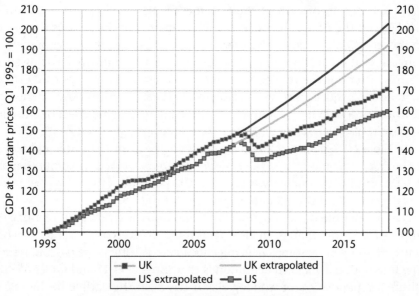

Data sources: ONS (ABMI) & NIPA Table 1.1.6.

Figure 1. UK and US: Decline in trend growth

Table 1. UK and US unemployment per cent Q4 2007 and Q4 2017 (Data sources: ONS (MGSX) and BLS (LNS 14000000))

	UK	US
Q4 2007	5.2	5.0
Q4 2017	4.4	4.1

works. In order to separate the impact of these variables, we need to know the number of people of working age, the ratio of those willing to work to this number, which is known as the participation rate, the rate of unemployment, and the number of hours worked per person employed. GDP can thus be broken down into the contribution of these different factors, and by comparing the changes over time we can assess their relative impact on the change in the rate of growth. For this purpose GDP can be measured in the following way:

GDP = Productivity × Hours worked

Hours worked = hours worked per person × numbers employed

Numbers employed = population of working age × participation rate
× employment rate

The contribution of each of these factors to the changes in the growth of the UK and the US can be isolated and compared for the periods leading up to the recession and during its aftermath. By measuring the effect of each we can assess their relative impact to determine why growth has slowed so sharply. I set out the results in Tables 1 to 5. From this analysis we can see that the two major causes of weak growth have been a slowing down in the rates at which productivity has improved and the demographic effect of a decline in the rate at which the populations of working age have been growing.

In Table 2 I separate changes in productivity from the other influences, including demography, on the number of hours worked. It shows that the deterioration in productivity equated to 102 per cent of the slowdown in the growth of GDP for the UK and 65 per cent for the US.

Having identified the contribution from productivity, I then identify the impact from the change in demography. Not everyone is able to work; some are too young, some are being educated, and others are old and retired. The internationally agreed definition is that those over 15 and under 65 constitute the population of working age; it has been the decline in the rate of growth of this group that has been the major cause of the slowdown in hours worked in both the UK and the US. If there had been no other changes then the fall in the numbers of people of working age would have caused GDP to slow in both countries, as I show in Table 3.

I use the internationally agreed definition for the participation rate, which is the number of those seeking work as a percentage of the population aged 15 to 65. Unfortunately the US Bureau of Labor Statistics (BLS) uses a different definition, which compares those seeking employment with the population, excluding those in jail or otherwise incarcerated, who are more than 16 years old. The BLS definition is thus unsuitable for analysis of the causes of slow growth. This is not only because the same definition needs to be used for both countries but also because the US definition excludes the impact of ageing and

Table 2. Changes in productivity and GDP comparing the period Q1 1995 to Q4 2007 with Q4 2007 to Q4 2017 (Data sources: ONS (ABMI and YBUS), US Bureau of the Census, NIPA Table 1.1.6 and BLS Table b 10)

	UK	US
Percentage change per annum in GDP Q1 1995 to Q4 2007 (A)	2.91	3.16
Percentage change per annum in GDP Q4 2007 to Q4 2017 (B)	1.04	1.43
Difference (C) = (B) minus (A)	−1.87	−1.73
Percentage change per annum in GDP per hour worked Q1 1995 to Q4 2007 (D)	2.10	1.93
Percentage change per annum in GDP per hour worked Q4 2007 to Q4 2017 (E)	0.19	0.82
Difference (F) = (E) minus (D)	−1.91	−1.12
(F) as percentage of (C)	101.8	64.6

Table 3. Changes in populations of working age and GDP comparing the period Q1 1995 to Q4 2007 with Q4 2007 to Q4 2017 (Data sources: ONS (ABMI), US Bureau of the Census and NIPA Table 1.1.6)

	UK	US
Percentage change per annum in population of working age Q1 1995 to Q4 2007 (A)	1.12	1.31
Percentage change per annum in population of working age Q4 2007 to Q4 2017 (B)	0.84	0.68
Extent to which the growth of GDP would have fallen in the absence of any other changes (C) = (B) minus (A)	−0.28	−0.64
Percentage change per annum in the growth of GDP (See Table 2) (D)	−1.87	−1.73
Contribution of demographic change to decline in growth (A) as percentage of (D)	15.0	36.7

Table 4. The combined impact (Data sources as in Tables 2 and 3)

	UK	US
Percentage contribution from labour productivity	101.8	64.6
Percentage contribution from demography	15.0	36.7
Combined impact (per cent)	116.8	102.3

consequent retirement. The BLS definition has often led to misleading press coverage through ignoring the impact of ageing, which has been the dominant influence on the change in the number of hours worked, comparing the periods before and after the financial crisis, in both the UK and the US.

Taken together, the changes in labour productivity and demography thus amount to more than 100 per cent of the slowdown in the growth rates of the UK and the US, comparing the two periods as I illustrate in Table 4.

Having identified the impact of productivity and demography on the change in the growth rates of GDP before and after the financial crisis, I assess the impact of the other factors. These are unemployment, hours worked per employee and the participation rate. Unemployment measures the numbers of people willing to work but unable to find jobs, while the participation rate measures the number of those willing to work (both employed and unemployed) as a proportion of those of working age.

The growth of GDP is determined by the rates of change of labour productivity and hours worked. Table 5 shows the contributions of each variable to the change in hours worked. In the UK the relative improvement between the two periods in the participation rate was nearly sufficient to offset the fall in numbers of people of working age, and with the help of relative changes in hours worked there was no net adverse effect on growth due to the impact of demography. The result is that the decline in UK growth can be attributed solely to the weakness of labour productivity.

Table 5. Impact of other factors on employment and hours worked comparing the two periods (Data sources: as previous Tables and ONS (MGSY and MGRZ) and BLS (LNS 14000000, LHS 13000000, and CES 000000001))

	UK	US
Contributions to changes in employment		
Percentage change in numbers of working age (A)	−0.44	−0.72
Percentage change in unemployment (B)	−0.19	0.04
Percentage change in participation rates (C)	0.39	0.06
Percentage change in numbers employed (D) = (A) + (B) + (C)	−0.23	−0.62
Add impact of change in hours worked per person		
Percentage changes in hours worked per person (E)	0.33	0.04
Percentage changes in hours worked (F) = (D) + (E)	0.09	−0.58

In the case of the US, however, participation rates and hours worked per person improved only marginally, so that even with some help from unemployment the slower growth of the working population in the second period had a significant impact on growth. The slowdown in growth that did not result from the relative change in labour productivity was 35.4 per cent of the total, and can be attributed to the fact that the relative decline in the growth of the numbers of working age was only slightly offset by the small improvements in the participation rate, hours worked per person, and numbers in employment.

It should be noted that the changes are not over the periods concerned but the differences between changes over the periods. For example, there were in the US significant improvements in unemployment in both periods, and so the considerable improvement during the second period shown in Table 1 had only a limited effect on the results shown in Table 5.

The change in demography had a greater impact on slowing growth in the US than in the UK, because it is not the speed at which the population of working age grows that has slowed growth but the change in that rate. This is often misunderstood. It is common to read that the US has been less affected by demographic factors than other mature economies, including the UK, because its population of those of working age is growing more rapidly. While this is correct if the actual rate of growth is being considered, it is wrong when changes in growth rates are the issue. The decline in the growth of the numbers of working age has been more marked in the US than in the UK and thus since the financial crisis it has slowed the growth of the US more than that of the UK.

As changes in productivity and demography have been responsible for the changes in the growth rates of the UK and US economies, the claim that the financial crisis has been responsible for the slowdown in growth can only be sustained if it caused the decline in either productivity or demography.

4

The Cause of Poor Productivity

Data on productivity, measured by the change in GDP per hours worked, have been available quarterly for the UK since 1971 and for the US since Q1 1964. Figure 2 for the UK and Figure 3 for the US show the change in productivity measured over five-year periods. I also mark on them, with a vertical line, the last quarter before the start of the recession, which was Q1 2008 for the UK and Q4 2007 for the US.

As Figure 2 and Figure 3 show,[1] the rate of improvement in productivity slowed sharply in both countries before the recession and has since fallen further. The fall in productivity in the recession provides no surprise, as employers are either unable or do not choose to reduce their employment as fast as demand falls. The fall that occurred before the recession indicates either a long-term trend or another of the periodic blips that have arisen in the past. But the lack of a bounce-back to previous levels indicates that the weakness in productivity shown before the recession is evidence of a long-term deterioration rather than a temporary one. The data therefore suggest that the decline in productivity in both the UK and the US predates the recession which followed the financial crisis.

The observation that the decline in productivity appears to have antedated the financial crisis does not prove that it cannot have been caused by it. Retail sales rise before Christmas but are nonetheless caused by Christmas, because everyone knows that it is coming. But it cannot be sensibly argued that the decline in productivity was caused by the subsequent crisis, not only because

---

[1] The figures for both UK and US labour productivity are calculated in Figures 2 and 3 by dividing GDP at constant prices by the number of hours worked. The data for the UK are published by the ONS (ABMI for GDP at constant prices) and (YBUS for hours worked). Those for US GDP at constant prices are published by the BEA (NIPA Table 1.1.6) and for hours worked by the BLS on their website (under bls.gov/pub/special requests/opt/table b 10). The BLS also publish a different quarterly figure for productivity (Id: PRS85006092) which is often quoted. But this is for the non-farm business sector only and thus does not relate to the whole economy. It should therefore not be used in conjunction with changes in GDP to calculate the contribution of changes in productivity to changes in economic growth.

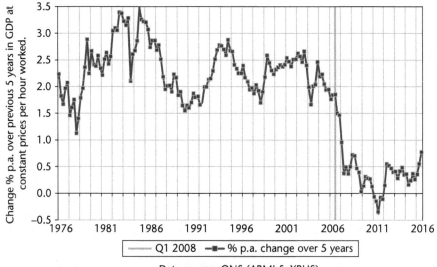

Data source: ONS (ABMI & YBUS).

Figure 2. UK: Labour productivity

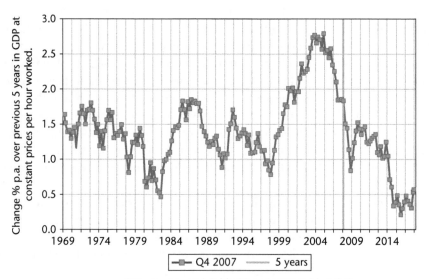

Data sources: BLS Table 10 and NIPA Table 1.1.6.

Figure 3. US: Labour productivity

the crisis was not expected but also because companies do not deliberately lower productivity if they expect either a crisis or a recession.

Productivity depends crucially on the amount and efficiency of the capital which employees operate. The speed at which productivity improves is thus largely determined by the rate at which the stock of capital grows and the

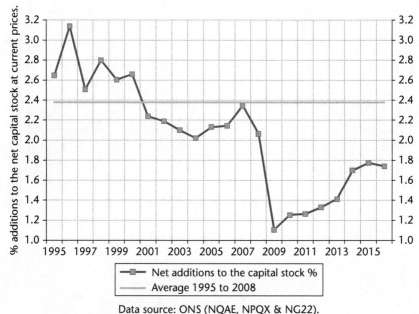

Data source: ONS (NQAE, NPQX & NG22).

Figure 4. UK: Net additions to the capital stock

efficiency of the capital in place. It thus depends on the level of past investment and, as new equipment is more efficient than old, when that investment occurred. Old equipment depreciates and the value of old investment therefore declines over time. The value of the net capital stock allows for such depreciation, and thus takes into account both the total amount of capital and its efficiency.

Data for the UK's net capital stock are currently available only from 1995 to 2016, but as Figure 4 shows, its growth fell sharply over this limited period and the decline had been sharp even before the recession of 2008.

In the US, for which we have data from 1925 to 2016, the growth of the net capital stock has been on a long declining trend since 1967, as shown in Figure 5. The recovery in the growth rate since the recession in 2009 appears to have stalled in 2016, at only 44 per cent of the long-term average level.

If these data correctly measure the value of the capital stock and thus allow for both its quantity and its efficiency, we should expect productivity to depend on its level. If we measure productivity by GDP per hour worked, we should expect it to have some stable relationship with the amount of the capital stock available to support each working hour and that GDP should have a stable relationship with the net capital stock.[2] We do not have

---

[2] If GDP/hour has a stable relationship with capital stock/hour, then GDP must have a stable relationship with the capital stock.

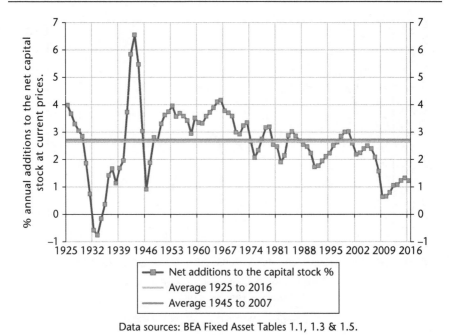

Data sources: BEA Fixed Asset Tables 1.1, 1.3 & 1.5.

Figure 5. US: Annual additions to the net capital stock

long-term data to test this hypothesis in the case of the UK but we do have it for the US and I show the ratios of the total and tangible capital stocks to GDP for the US in Figure 6.

As Figure 6 shows, the net tangible and total capital/output ratios clearly rotate around a stable average and they are therefore mean-reverting. The hypothesis that productivity depends on the level of the net capital stock per hour worked is thus testable for the US and robust when tested. Although we lack sufficient data to be able to test this for the UK, the assumption on which the hypothesis is based is just as applicable to the UK as it is to the US and it is therefore reasonable to assume that it is valid for both countries.

As GDP has the stable relationship with the net capital stock shown in Figure 6, we must expect the rate at which productivity changes to be related to the rate at which the net capital stock/per hour worked changes. Figure 7 illustrates that this expectation is fully met.[3] The data therefore make it clear that the reason that productivity has improved so slowly is the weak growth in the net capital stock. Figures 4 and 5 show that the declines in the growth of

---

[3] Both changes are measured at current prices, and while they are comparable in relative terms they do not show the rates at which productivity has grown if measured in constant prices. The R^2 correlations between the growth of the net capital stock per hour and productivity are 0.57, 0.70, 0.75, 0.77, and 0.79 measured over the past one to five years.

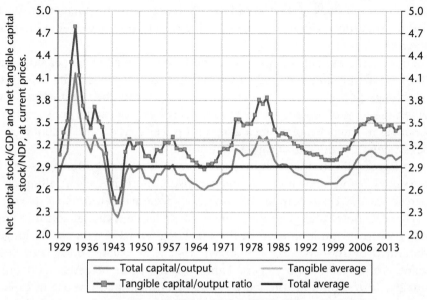

Data sources: NIPA Table 1.1.5 & BEA Fixed Asset Table 1.1.

Figure 6. US: Capital/output ratios

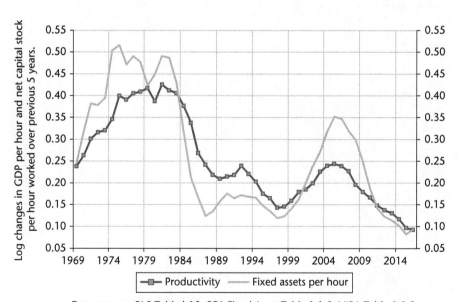

Data sources: BLS Table b10, BEA Fixed Asset Table 1.1 & NIPA Table 1.1.5.

Figure 7. US: Changes in productivity and net capital stock per hour worked

the net capital stock of the UK and the US long predate the financial crisis. It follows that the weakness in labour productivity cannot have been caused by the financial crisis.

Figure 7 shows that the growth of the US net capital stock per hour has declined sharply and that productivity has subsequently fallen with it. Subject to changes in the value of the existing stock of capital, the net stock will rise when the level of gross investment exceeds the rate of capital consumption. Changes in the net capital stock at current prices thus depend on both gross investment and the rate of capital consumption.

As Figure 8 illustrates, gross investment, which included intangibles and is measured before allowing for capital consumption, has been falling as a percentage of GDP in both the US and the UK for the past thirty to forty years.

Figure 9 shows that gross investment has fallen and capital consumption has risen over the long term in the US. Long-term UK data are no longer published by the ONS. Figure 9 shows what is available, and it is of little value as it covers too short a period and is (as the figure suggests) of doubtful quality. In the US both the fall in gross investment and the rise in capital consumption have contributed to the slowdown in the rate at which the net capital stock has risen, and this is also likely to be the case in the UK—though the data are not available to confirm this. In the US (Figure 10) net investment is less than half peak levels.

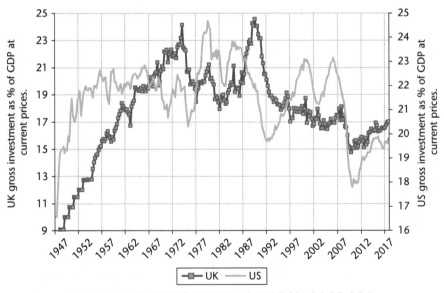

Data sources: ONS (NPQS & YBHA) and NIPA Tables 1.1.5 & 3.9.5.

Figure 8. UK and US: Gross fixed investment

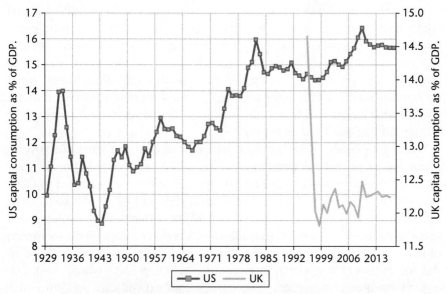

Data sources: ONS (YBHA & NQAE) and NIPA Tables 1.1.5 & 5.1.

Figure 9. UK and US: Capital consumption as percentage of GDP

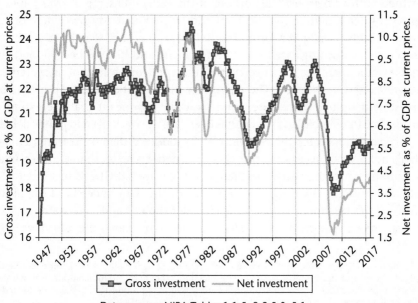

Data sources: NIPA Tables 1.1.5, 3.9.5 & 5.1.

Figure 10. US: Gross and net investment

Investment takes two main forms: tangible assets, such as buildings and equipment, and intangible assets, such as money spent on research and development (R&D). The rate of capital consumption varies between different types of tangible assets and with changes in the proportion of tangible to intangible investment. For example, in the case of tangible investment capital consumption will be faster for an oil well with a short production life than for a well with a longer one. In general, however, tangible investment tends to be written off less quickly than intangible.

When people don't like the data they seek to change them, and governments are particularly anxious to show that GDP has been rising under their watch. There have been several recent changes in the measurement of GDP, which have resulted in it appearing to be higher and its growth faster than shown by the previous method. It should be noted that data for earlier as well as for more recent years have been adjusted. A recent example is the treatment of investment, which has been increased by the inclusion of expenditure on the acquisition of intellectual property (IP) including R&D, which was previously treated as intermediate rather than final expenditure and thus (like advertising) as a cost of being in business.[4] Some claim that these adjustments do not go far enough and that, for example, advertising expenditure should also be treated as investment.[5] The argument for including advertising is very similar to that for including R&D[6] and it therefore seems reasonable to include both or neither. The authors of the Federal Reserve Board's paper to which I refer conclude that both should be included. My own view is that including advertising as a form of investment should be seen to be so absurd as to provide a strong case for both advertising and R&D to be excluded and that it would therefore have been better if the previous system of measurement had remained unchanged. The change in the definition of much intangible investment from intermediate to final output has meant that the extent of the decline in tangible investment has been largely overlooked in public debate.

Different models for the economy will produce different measurements of GDP, and it is not necessarily true that one model is better than another. In an important sense, therefore, the change in the way that GDP is measured does not really matter, provided that the users of the data understand the differences in the treatment of investment under the old and new systems. Such measurement changes do not really improve GDP or alter the rate at which it

[4] The distinction is important to avoid double counting in the output data. For example the output of steel and automobiles should not be added together to record total output, as much steel is used to produce motor cars. The amount of steel used in car production is therefore treated as intermediate rather than final expenditure.

[5] See for example Corrado, Hulten, and Sichel (2009).

[6] Basically it is argued that companies would not indulge in either advertising or R&D unless they expected to benefit from these expenditures in the future and they should therefore be considered as forms of investment.

Data sources: ONS (DLXP & NPQS) and NIPA Tables 1.1.5 & 3.9.5.

Figure 11. UK and US: Intangible investment as percentage of total investment

changes. We will not make voters any less dissatisfied by telling them that their living standards are rising when they think they have been falling. To improve welfare we need to make GDP per head rise without changing the way it is measured.

As Figure 11 shows, investment in IP has grown in the US from 3 per cent of total gross investment in 1929 and 7 per cent in 1948 to 25 per cent in 2016. UK data are only available since 1987. Net investment has fallen more than gross due to a rise in capital consumption, which is not necessarily the result of the rise in intangible investment shown in Figure 10, though that has probably been the most important factor.

Because intangible investment is written off relatively quickly, the changes in net investment shown in Figure 10 for the UK and Figure 11 for the US largely reflect those that occurred in tangible investment. I illustrate the close relationship in Figure 12 for the UK and Figure 13 for the US. The relationship in closer for the US than for the UK, probably because the estimate for capital consumption is much more volatile in the case of the UK.

Before the changes in the way gross investment is measured, the growth of the capital stock was much more closely associated with the level of gross investment than it is today. The changes do not seem to have been fully appreciated in public debate: there has thus been a tendency to overlook the extent to which net investment has fallen and hence a failure to notice the association with the decline in growth and productivity.

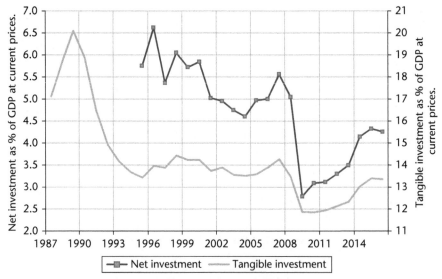

Data source: ONS (DLYP, YBHA, NPQS & NQAE).

Figure 12. UK: Net and tangible investment

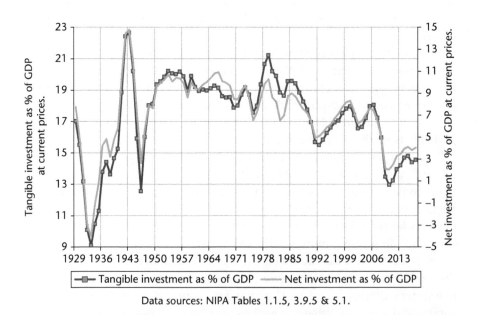

Data sources: NIPA Tables 1.1.5, 3.9.5 & 5.1.

Figure 13. US: Net and tangible investment

The decline in productivity was preceded by a marked slowdown in the rate at which additions were made to the capital stock. As Figures 6 and 7 show, the growth in output depends on the growth in the value of the capital stock. As investment has weakened the growth in the capital stock has fallen, and this is clearly why productivity has been so poor. This does not mean that there cannot be improvements in the short-term, since the ratio of output to the value of the net capital stock, while mean-reverting, is not fixed from year to year.

The decline in net investment has received insufficient attention, but it has not gone entirely unnoticed. Robert Gordon, who is probably the most prominent of the economists who have written about productivity, has drawn attention to the fall in the growth of the net capital stock, as I do in Figure 5,[7] and Mervyn King, the former Governor of the Bank of England, remarked that the main reason for the disappointment over productivity 'is that there has been a sharp fall in the growth rate and perhaps even the level of the effective capital stock in the economy'.[8]

As GDP revolves around a stable ratio to the value of the net capital stock (Figure 6), productivity depends on the level of that capital stock per hour worked. Improving productivity thus requires increasing the growth rate of the net capital stock, either by increasing the level of investment or reducing the rate of capital consumption. As tangible capital is consumed at a slower pace than intangible, this amounts to increasing the level of tangible investment; unless this happens productivity is unlikely to improve.

Productivity is, however, unlikely to increase by as much as the rise in gross tangible investment, because depreciation, which constitutes a major part of capital consumption, increases with productivity.[9] New capital has embedded in it the technology of its time. After new capital has been installed its output per hour is thus unlikely to change much, at least after those working with it have become fully acquainted with its capabilities. The return on the recently installed equipment will then fall over time as real wages rise. If the labour share of output is stable, real wages will rise with productivity. The stability of the net capital/output ratio (Figure 6) does not therefore imply that productivity will rise proportionately with increased tangible investment, but it does mean that a rise in tangible investment is likely to be a necessary condition for a rise in productivity.

As the rate at which productivity improves has a direct impact on the speed at which real wages rise, the speed at which the profitability and thus value of old equipment falls varies with productivity. Although changes in productivity are not directly used to value the capital stock or the rate of depreciation,

---

[7] Gordon (2016).   [8] King (2016).   [9] Solow, Tobin, von Weizsacker and Yaari (1966).

the use of survey data for both ensures that productivity is in practice an essential determinant of value as shown in the official data.[10]

The key message from the data is that tangible investment had been weak for many years before the recession of 2008 but because of the increase in the investment in intangibles the extent of the decline has been largely overlooked.

---

[10] See Appendix 2 for details of the approach of both the ONS and the BEA to valuing the capital stock and rates of depreciation.

5

Ageing Populations

The changes in demography, together with low investment and poor productivity, have been responsible for the whole of the decline in the trend growth rates of the UK and US economies, even when compensating factors are taken into account.

Figure 14 shows the way in which the numbers of those of working age have changed in recent years and the way this is expected to change in the future. In both the UK and the US there has been a sharp decline in growth of the population aged 15 to 65 since the financial crisis started in 2007. But this is a coincidental not a causal connection. The slowdown in the growth of the working age population after the financial crisis was due to the fall in the birth rate that occurred in both countries after the post-war baby boom ended.

Figure 15 illustrates the high birth rates in the UK and the US in the immediate post-war period and the sharp decline that occurred from around 1960 onwards. The lower birth rate caused a decline in the numbers of those entering the workforce fifteen to twenty years later. For many years this was balanced by the fact that the earlier rise in the birth rate was still boosting the numbers of those in their fifties and sixties, but in time the baby boomers began to retire and, as the birth rate remained low, we have now entered a period in which the native born workforce will grow much more slowly than it has over the previous sixty years.

A rise in the number of immigrants could change this pattern, as they are predominantly of working age. But without a major change in the willingness of voters in the UK and the US to accept an even greater inflow than has occurred in recent years, the much reduced growth in those of working age is likely to continue as shown in Figure 14.

Living standards measured by GDP per person are given a boost when the population of working age grows faster than the total population. This favourable change in demography was the situation up to 2008. Until then living standards tended to improve faster than productivity. Since then the total population has been growing faster than the numbers of working age

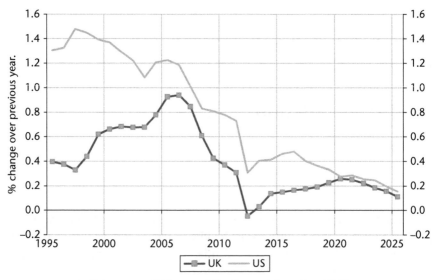

Data source: US Bureau of the Census International Tables.

Figure 14. UK and US: Population of working age (those aged between 15 and 65)

Data sources: UK & US Censuses.

Figure 15. UK and US: The post-war baby boom

and living standards will now tend to grow less rapidly than productivity. The impact on prosperity has been sharp because we have moved from a favourable to an unfavourable situation. The gap between the rate of growth of the population aged 15 to 65 and that of the total population is known as

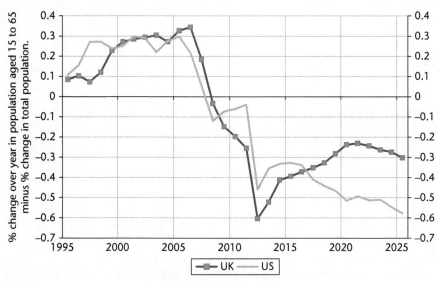

Data source: US Bureau of the Census.

Figure 16. UK and US: Demographic surpluses and deficits

the demographic surplus, if the numbers of working age grow faster than the total population, or the demographic deficit, if the growth is slower.

I illustrate this in Figure 16. Prior to 2008 there were demographic surpluses in both countries but these then changed to deficits, which are expected to continue for many years ahead. We have therefore changed from a world in which living standards tended to grow faster than productivity to one in which they will grow more slowly. The demographic deficit is such that in the absence of other changes, in 2017 productivity would have needed to grow by 0.4 per cent in both countries to prevent living standards from falling. This deficit is subsequently expected to moderate in the UK but to become even worse in the US, where it is forecast to rise to over 0.5 per cent per annum in the US from 2020 to 2025. The demographic challenge is thus even greater for the US than for the UK.

Population estimates can of course err. Birth rates are particularly hard to forecast accurately, but it takes fifteen years for changing birth rates to have an impact on the size of the workforce, so a significant change in the demographic deficit is unlikely without a large rise in immigrants, who are predominantly of working age. Currently, however, such a rise looks unlikely, as on both sides of the Atlantic there is increasing popular opposition to faster immigration.

6

Other Influences on Growth

Productivity and demography have been the major determinants of growth and this will continue unless there are significant favourable changes in unemployment, hours worked, and participation rates.

As Figure 17 shows, unemployment levels are now below their long-term averages. Changes are therefore unlikely to provide much further help to growth, even if unemployment in the UK and the US can fall further for a while without increasing inflationary pressure.

Hours worked per employee have, as Figure 18 illustrates, shown a long-term falling trend. Though they also fell in the recent recession they then recovered, illustrating the natural cyclical response of companies to a fall in demand which they hope will not be permanent and to which they are therefore reluctant to respond by laying off employees. The long-term fall in hours worked probably represents a preference for increased leisure as living standards have risen. As future rises in living standards are, sadly, unlikely, it would seem overly pessimistic to assume that the longer-term trend for working hours per person to fall will continue. Changes in hours worked per employee will probably have little impact on future growth.

The proportion of women of working age who are employed is lower than that of men. The gap narrowed sharply following World War II as the proportion of women who were employed outside the home rose steadily. This has now tended to stabilize, so that the long-term rise in participation rates from this source has largely ended.

The post-1995 trend has been for participation rates to rise in the UK and fall in the US. As I show in Figure 19, between Q1 1995 and Q1 2017 the UK participation rate rose at 0.33 per cent per annum and that of the US fell at 0.02 per cent per annum. As an increasing number of those over 65 seem likely to choose to work for at least a few more years, there is clearly scope for the participation rates to rise in both countries. Government action can encourage this, one way being to delay the age at which pensions are paid.

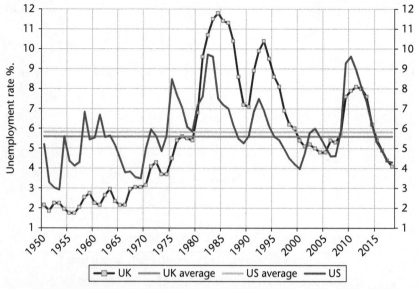

Data sources: ONS (MGSX) + C.H.Feinstein (pre-1971) & BLS (14000000).

Figure 17. UK and US: Post-war unemployment

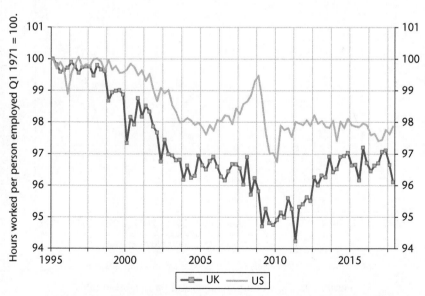

Data sources: ONS (MGRZ & YBUS) and BLS (Table 10 & CES0000000001).

Figure 18. UK and US: Hours worked per employee

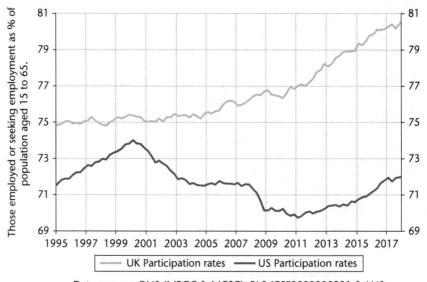

Data sources: ONS (MRGC & MCSC), BLS (CSE0000000001 & LNS 13000000) and US Census Bureau.

Figure 19. UK and US: Participation rates

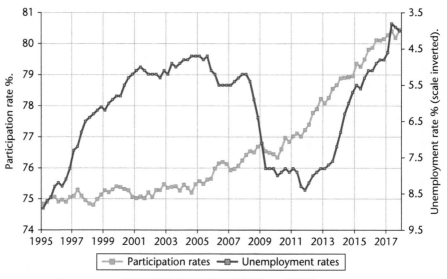

Data sources: ONS (MRGC, MGSX & MCSC), and US Census Bureau.

Figure 20. UK: Unemployment and participation rates

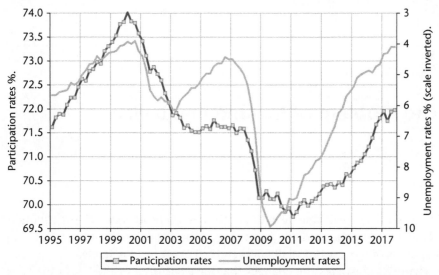

Data sources: BLS (CSE0000000001, LNS 13000000 & LNS 14000000) and US Census Bureau.

Figure 21. US: Unemployment and participation rates

In both countries participation has tended to move with unemployment, as I show in Figure 20 for the UK and Figure 21 for the US, though the pattern is less clear for the UK. (I have inverted the scale for unemployment to make the relationship more obvious to the eye.) As further falls in unemployment are improbable, improvements in participation rates are likely to be limited.

It does not therefore seem likely that either unemployment, hours worked, or participation rates are likely to change in ways that will significantly boost the trend growth rates of either the UK or the US. As demography is also unlikely to change, all hope of boosting growth must rest on productivity.

7

The Problem of Income Inequality

Living standards will change in line with GDP per head only if the distribution of incomes is unchanged. If incomes become less equally distributed the living standards of most people will fall even if GDP per head is stable.

Figure 22 illustrates the changes that have occurred in the UK in the Gini Coefficient, the most widely used indicator designed to measure the distribution of household income.[1] A rise in this coefficient denotes an increase in inequality of income. The figure shows that inequality, on this measure, has risen overall since 1977 but stabilized after 1987, falling in more recent years.

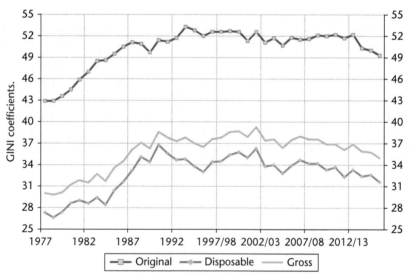

Data source: ONS (From Figure 12 Effects of Taxes & Benefits on UK Household Income.)

Figure 22. UK: Gini Coefficient (measure of household income inequality)

---

[1] See Appendix 3 for an explanation as to how this is calculated.

Data source: US Bureau of the Census (partly by inspection from chart).

Figure 23. US: Gini Coefficient (measure of household income inequality)

Figure 23 illustrates the changes in the Gini Coefficient for the US. This shows a long-term increase in income inequality, though it is exaggerated in the figure owing to a change in 1993 in the way the data were calculated. However, the direction of change is clear, since the trend was rising both in the period 1967 to 1993 and from 1993 onwards.

Another way of way of assessing the change in income inequality is to compare the mean—the average income per person—with the median, which is the level at which the numbers of those with higher incomes per household and those with lower are equal. If the growth rate of the median income is slower than that of the mean, then the majority of people in an economy will have falling real incomes even if GDP per head is stable. This is useful when considering the political impact of economic change, as the median income provides a guide to the way in which the living standards of the average voter have changed.

I have been unable to find these data for the UK, but Table 6 compares the changes in US mean and median incomes from 1975 to 2013 and the two sub-periods 1975 to 1995 and 1995 to 2013. On this measure there was a rise in US inequality throughout the whole period, and, though there was some moderation in the second sub-period compared with the first, the negative impact on living standards was greater because of the marked slow-down in the growth of average incomes.

Table 6. Percentage changes per annum in US median and average incomes (Data source: US Bureau of the Census)

	1975 to 2013	1975 to 1995	1995 to 2013
Mean household income	0.77	1.15	0.35
Median household income	0.29	0.54	0.02
Mean minus median	0.47	0.61	0.33

Unless this US trend for increased income inequality halts, the threat to most people's living standards will be greater than simply considering average incomes might imply. It is quite likely therefore that even if GDP per head rises in the US, the living standard of the typical voter will fall. The recent data suggest changes in income inequality pose less of a threat to living standards in the UK than in the US.

In the previous chapter I showed that the outlook for GDP per head is unlikely to differ much from what is worryingly indicated by looking at productivity and demography. An increase in inequality adds to the threat to most people's living standards. I am not seeking to forecast how living standards will change. The scope for good and ill fortune is too great to make this, in my view, a sensible exercise. My purpose is to show the extent of the threat we face. It is, therefore, important to understand that if the recent trends in productivity and income inequality do not improve, the living standards of most people in the UK and the US may well fall and at best are unlikely to meet voters' expectations.

When asked what to do when driven onto a lea shore with loss of power, sailing manuals tell us that there is one and only one solution: 'Do not allow this situation to arise.' We should attend to the sailing manuals' advice. We are threatened with a sustained fall in the real incomes of most people and we must not allow this situation to arise.

8

Two Models of Growth

To avoid stagnation we must boost growth. The question for policy is whether we must rely on improvements in technology, which appears hard to accelerate, or can enhance growth by encouraging additional investment. To decide on the appropriate policy we must therefore understand the way growth is determined and, in particular, must separate the contribution of technology from other factors.

It is both reasonable and generally accepted that growth depends on changes in the supply of capital, labour and technology. This is the basis for the growth accounting framework set out by Robert Solow.[1] I shall follow this but differ from the standard consensus interpretation of Solow's model that has evolved over time and has been set out in a manual published by the OECD.[2] Both my model and the standard approach calculate the volumes of capital and labour and their contributions to growth, with the residual being the contribution from Total Factor Productivity (TFP). The results of the two approaches are significantly different and, even more importantly, they suggest different policies. The standard approach has encouraged the belief that policy can do little to encourage growth. This pessimism is reflected in what has become known as Endogenous Growth Theory. My model is optimistic as it shows that growth can be advanced, by encouraging additional investment, beyond the rate that results from changes in technology alone. This is particularly relevant today when changes in management remuneration have discouraged investment and held back growth.

My fundamental objection to the models which follow the OECD Manual is that they are untestable and therefore unscientific. I shall term these as the standard or consensus approaches. In contrast to them I show that my own model is not only testable but is robust when tested and should therefore be preferred. There are two key differences in the models which produce

---

[1] Solow (1956).   [2] OECD (2009).

this divergence: the way in which capital volumes are calculated, and the influences other than technology which determine the level of investment and the capital stock.

When measuring capital the standard approach holds that old equipment not only depreciates but decays and that it is therefore wrong to use survey data on the volume of the capital stock. I think that this is a mistake. While it is right that volume measures of the capital stock do not measure productive capacity, it does not follow that they are somehow invalid. The objection to volume measures would only obtain if it were assumed that productivity of the existing capital stock remained unchanged until the stock was scrapped. No such assumption is made in my model.

I have a fundamental objection to the use in the standard model of capital services as a way of calculating the volume of the net capital stock. Capital services are a flow and flows can be valued by discounting the amounts for individual years at some assumed rate of interest. But this unavoidably provides a measure of value, and I fail to see how it can produce a measure of volume.

It is also helpful to observe that equipment which is properly maintained does not decay but remains as efficient as ever. It is less efficient than new equipment because it embodies older technology, not because its efficiency has necessarily weakened over time. Equipment depreciates even if it does not decay, but this is largely (though not exclusively) because the returns on it fall as real wages rise with improving labour productivity.[3] The rate of depreciation thus varies with fluctuations in labour productivity. Of course, at any stage in its life equipment may not be properly maintained. However, for the purposes of measuring volume it does not matter whether the efficiency of old capital falls relative to new through variations in the impact of new technology or through the lack of sufficient maintenance.

The OECD Manual points out that the volume of capital can be assessed as a stock or as the source of a flow. It rejects the stock approach on the grounds (which I consider invalid) that 'capital decay is a fact'. This has several consequences. It means that the data on the capital volume as produced by the Office of National Statistics (ONS) in the UK and the Bureau of Economic Analysis (BEA) in the US are ignored. It requires assumptions about cost to arrive at an estimate of capital volume, which seem to me to make it a measure of value and not of volume—and which then invalidates models that seek to assess the contribution to growth from changes in the volume of capital.

My model avoids these problems in calculating the volume of the capital stock by using official data. The approaches of the ONS and the BEA are

---

[3] In this respect my model follows the work of Robert Solow: see Solow, Tobin, von Weizsacker, and Yaari (1966).

basically the same. The volume and value of the capital stock are, respectively, the original cost of all equipment that has not been scrapped and the price at which the equipment can currently be sold.[4] Neither the ONS nor the BEA publish the results of their surveys of the volume of the capital stock directly and the available ONS data cover only the past twenty years, which is too short a period to be useful. The BEA, however, publish data on the average age of the capital stock since 1925 and this, combined with their NIPA data on tangible investment, has allowed me to calculate the volume of the US capital stock—making only one assumption, which is that older equipment is scrapped before newer.

The second major difference between the standard approach and mine concerns the influences other than technology which determine investment. The standard approach assumes that these can be lumped together as the cost of capital, while I treat them separately as 'non-technology variables' (NTVs). These two concepts are similar and could under certain definitions be the same. In practice they are not. The consensus approach to the return on capital uses a model in which debt, equity, leverage and corporation tax are excluded, with the return on capital being measured before interest and tax are deducted. One problem arising from this is that the central importance of the return on equity is overlooked. Corporate investment appears to be heavily influenced by the need for new capital to be sufficiently profitable for the return on equity to exceed the required hurdle rate. This is shown by the great attention paid by stock market investors and analysts to corporate returns on equity. If returns on capital are calculated before depreciation interest and tax, small differences in them become large differences in the return on equity, both because the profits after tax have averaged only 28 per cent of those measured before capital consumption, interest and tax (Figure 24) and because less equity has been required to finance output as leverage has risen (Figure 25).

The exclusion of equity in the standard approach to the cost of capital is a vital defect. The combined cost of the two sources of capital—debt and equity—is dominated by the latter, because debt interest is allowed as a cost for corporation tax and because returns on equity are higher than those on debt. By not treating equity separately and assuming that investment responds to changes in the cost of capital, the consensus approach assumes that changes in the cost of equity will impact the level of investment. I will show that this is, however, demonstrably incorrect and invalidates the consensus model in that one of its basic assumptions is testable and wrong. Another shortcoming in the standard approach that has led to critical

---

[4] Details of the ONS and BEA methods are set out in Appendix 2.

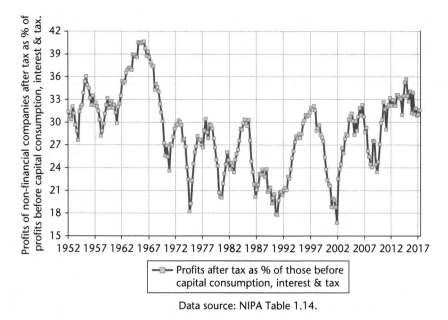

Data source: NIPA Table 1.14.

Figure 24. US: Non-financial companies' profits after tax as percentage of broadly defined profits

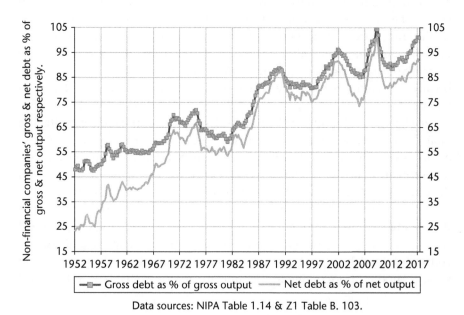

Data sources: NIPA Table 1.14 & Z1 Table B. 103.

Figure 25. US: Non-financial corporate leverage

comment arises from differing estimates of the cost of capital. 'Fairly innocu-ous differences in assumptions can lead to very different estimates of TFP growth.'[5] By excluding so many variables included in NTV the standard model implicitly assumes that the capital stock does not respond to changes in leverage and the hurdle rate (the minimum return on equity needed by managements to justify investment).

The consensus definition of the cost of capital follows the work of Hall and Jorgensen.[6] In their model there is no corporate veil: investors benefit from buying capital which they rent out and then sell, and their return is the rent minus the depreciation. But investment does not appear to follow a pattern consistent with these assumptions. If it did, it would be mainly driven by the cost of equity: however, there appears to be no relationship between the two. Both the data and anecdotal evidence indicate that companies' investment is determined by the need for the return on equity to at least equal the hurdle rate.

It is unlikely that the apparent thickness of the corporate veil could be maintained if the behaviour of companies were contrary to the interests of their shareholders. The Hall–Jorgensen model implicitly assumes that share-holders would benefit if the amount of corporate capital responded to its cost. But shareholders are concerned with their wealth, not with the value of capital of the companies they own, and there is in practice a large difference between the two. Over the time horizons with which they are concerned, shareholders do not benefit from the value of the companies in which they invest but only from their share prices. If companies were to respond by raising add-itional equity when it is cheap, they would reduce share prices and thus current shareholder wealth.

Returns to shareholders on US equities appear to be stable in the long-term, fluctuating around 6 per cent per annum in real terms, as illustrated in Figure 26. As over time the return on equity to investors must be the same as the return on corporate equity, the long-term real hurdle rate must also be around 6 per cent per annum.

This long-term stability also allows the US equity market to be valued either (as proposed by Robert Shiller[7]) using the cyclically adjusted price–earnings ratio or (as proposed by Stephen Wright and me[8]) using the q ratio of market to replacement value. As Figure 27 shows, these two approaches give the same result for the swings in equity prices around their equilibrium value.

As the long-term return on equity is stable the long-term cost of raising new equity varies around 6 per cent depending on the level of the stock market. As Figure 28 shows, companies do not appear to respond in terms of investment

---

[5] Ghosh and Kraay (2000).   [6] Hall and Jorgensen (1967).   [7] Shiller (2000).
[8] Smithers and Wright (2000).

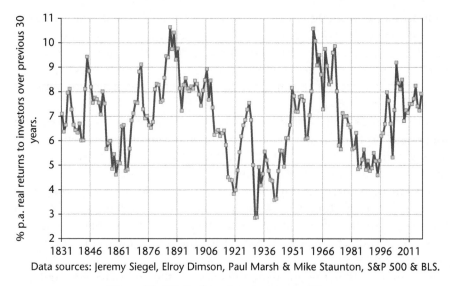

Data sources: Jeremy Siegel, Elroy Dimson, Paul Marsh & Mike Staunton, S&P 500 & BLS.

Figure 26. US: Real equity returns over 30 years

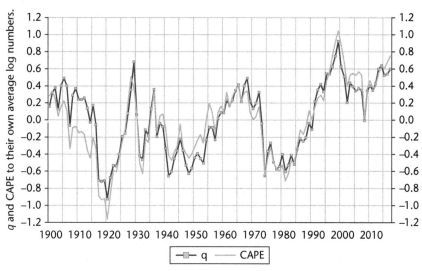

Data sources: For *q* Stephen Wright 1900 to 1945 & Federal Reserve Z1 Table B. 103 to Q3 2017. For CAPE Robert Shiller updated.

Figure 27. US stock market value according to *q* and CAPE

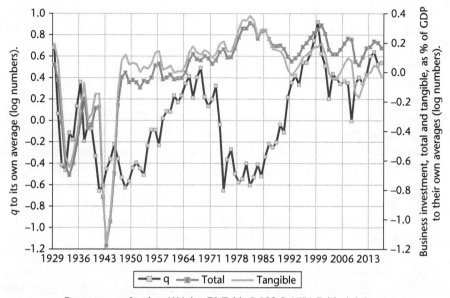

Data sources: Stephen Wright, Z1 Table B.103 & NIPA Table 1.1.5.

Figure 28. US: Business investment and the cost of equity

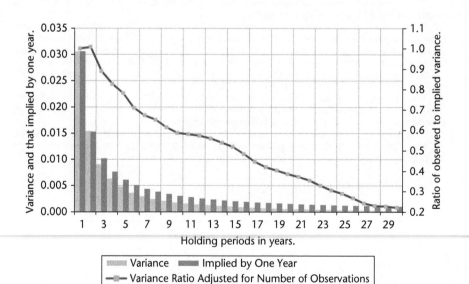

Data sources: Siegel, Dimson, et al. S&P 500 & BLS.

Figure 29. US Equities: Annual volatility and returns 1801 to 2016

to the cost of equity which has the predominant impact on the total cost of capital. This applies to the economy as a whole, as business is responsible for the major part of all investment.[9]

The variables that determine whether or not a given investment will produce a sufficient return to pass the hurdle rate include profit margins, leverage, interest rates and the level of corporation tax. These therefore need to be included in a valid model which seeks to identify the contributions to growth from volume changes in capital and labour and the residual attributable to TFP.

The ability to value the stock market depends on the returns from it not being random but mean-reverting. This can be demonstrated not only by the history of those returns shown in Figure 26 but by the way in which the volatility of real equity returns, as shown in Figure 29, declines over time and declines much faster than it would solely as a result of being measured over a longer period.[10] It is not just because the same degree of short-term volatility would have less impact on the total return the longer an investment is held, but also because volatility declines over time This shows that stock market returns are not random;[11] after periods when they have been high, real returns tend to fall and, when they have been low, to rise.[12]

---

[9] The R^2 correlations between investment as a percentage of GDP and q are 0.10 for total investment and 0.01 for tangible investment.

[10] If we had an infinite number of observations and returns followed a random walk the ratio between the actual and implied variance would always be one. If we have T observations then the expected variance ratio at year n would be $(T - n + 1)/T$. I have therefore adjusted the ratio for the number of observations. A virtually identical pattern to that of Figure 26 is shown if volatilities are measured over different periods: for example, if the data are restricted separately to either the nineteenth or the twentieth century.

[11] More precisely they do not follow a 'random walk with drift'. Even if past returns had no impact on future returns, equities would still give a positive long-term real return, and the value of an equity portfolio would still have a positive upward drift.

[12] This is known as negative serial correlation. Its existence in this context is confirmed by the fact that almost exactly the same pattern as that illustrated in Figure 26 is shown for non-overlapping sub-periods such as the nineteenth and twentieth centuries.

9

Investment and the Stock of Capital

Investment in intangibles does not increase the volume of the capital stock, nor is it designed to do so. The aim is to increase the efficiency of tangible investment. The volume of the capital stock must therefore be represented by tangible capital; intangible assets such as those that arise from investment in research and development (R&D) and other forms of intellectual products (IP) must be excluded. As I have already pointed out, before 2013 in both the UK and the US most investment in IP was treated as being intermediate rather than final expenditure and thus, like advertising, a cost of being in business rather than a form of investment. The change to defining IP investment as a final output has had the unfortunate effect of limiting public awareness about the extent to which tangible investment has fallen. (I should however emphasize that for the purposes of measuring the volume of the capital stock it does not matter whether IP is treated as a final or intermediate expenditure, so long as it is excluded from the volume measure of capital.)

Measuring the volume of capital exclusively in terms of tangible assets has the additional advantage of excluding data of dubious accuracy. In the US a large tax credit for R&D was introduced in 1981. Figure 30 shows that private sector spending on IP averaged 12 per cent of total investment for twenty-five years before that and has since risen to over 30 per cent. Over the same period TFP, as measured by either the consensus model or mine, has deteriorated. Therefore, if the data on IP investment are correct, it has been singularly unproductive. The more likely alternative is that the rise in the amount attributed to R&D investment in the national accounts does not represent the extent to which expenditure on research has actually increased, but is mainly due to a reclassification of spending. Anecdotal evidence points to companies 'gaming the system' by categorizing an increasing part of the salaries and other costs of employees, previously treated as general expenditure, as being investment in R&D. If the data used by companies in their tax returns are treated by the national accountants as being a fair measure of R&D expenditure, the result will be a rise in investment and GDP as shown

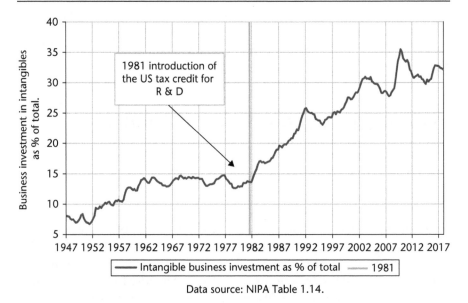

Data source: NIPA Table 1.14.

Figure 30. US: Intangible business investment as percentage of total business investment

in the data, but which does not necessarily represent a real increase. It appears that either expenditure on R&D is ineffective in improving TFP or it is mismeasured.

Certainly there is strong anecdotal evidence that investment in IP is mismeasured. The tax credit encourages companies to redefine expenditure previously allocated to general management as R&D, and if this is done and accepted by the tax authorities and the national accountants as representing a true rise, then the data will be distorted.

An alternative view is expressed by Charles Hulten:

> Neoclassical growth models assume that innovation is an exogenous process, with the implication that investments in R&D have no systematic and predictable effect on output growth. But, can it really be true that the huge amount of R&D investment was made in recent years without any expectation of gain? A more plausible approach is to abandon the assumption that innovation is exogenous to the economic system and recognize that some part of innovation is, in fact, a form of capital accumulation.[1]

It seems to me that it is more plausible to assume that the gain expected from recording the huge amount of R&D expenditure has been in the form of a reduction in tax rather than an improvement in technology. It is naive to

---

[1] Hulten (2001).

believe that when there is a large tax credit for R&D, the only benefit from claims made for such spending comes from accelerated innovation.

A valid model must be capable of being tested. The results of the consensus approach do not appear to be so; furthermore, some of the assumptions underlying the model are testable and, when tested, are not robust.

10

Description of My Model

It is agreed in both the standard approach and my model that investment is needed to allow improvements in technology to affect the economy and that the amount of this investment will be determined by other influences, so that its level is the point on the graph for current technology, which corresponds to the weight of those other influences.

In my model the volume of the capital stock is defined as the original cost at constant prices of all tangible fixed capital that has not been scrapped. ONS data for volume are not published and even value data are only available since 1987. I am forced therefore to limit the calculations and testing of my model to the US.[1] For the volume of labour I use the data on civilian employment. Both labour and capital can improve in quality as well as change in volume; my model treats quality improvements in both as part of TFP. This is simpler and avoids the difficulty of measuring improvements in the quality of labour. I am not, however, suggesting that rising levels of education and other improvements in the quality of labour are unimportant: indeed, they may be essential for allowing improvements in capital efficiency to be implemented.

Productivity varies with the level of unemployment, and the model seeks to determine the level of TFP independent of such fluctuations and thus to measure changes in TFP on the basis of an economy operating at full employment.

The contribution of capital and labour to the growth of output will remain the same if there is no improvement in technology. Suppose the volumes of labour and capital change at the same rate, then if technology is unchanged, output will expand at this rate but labour productivity will be unchanged,[2]

---

[1] The volume data on the capital stock are derived from the BEA's Fixed Asset Table 1.9 and data on past investment from NIPA Tables 1.1.4, 1.1.5, and 3.9.5.
[2] In combination labour and capital have constant returns to scale.

while a change in technology will be manifested as an improvement in labour productivity. Growth comes from investment responding either to changes in NTV or changes in technology (TFP). If the sole cause is TFP, then the volume of the capital stock will rise in line with the volume of labour. Differences in the growth rates of labour and the capital stock will thus be due to changes in NTV.

All capital uses some technology. At any given time the amount of capital in use will depend on the overall level of technology and the amount that can be financed, as illustrated in Figure 31. The state of technology at different times is shown by (T 1) and (T 2).

Provided that the constituents of NTV do not change in ways that automatically neutralize each other, the amount of capital that can be financed at any one time will depend on NTV, which must therefore be exogenous. That it is, at least over the time period being considered, is shown in Figure 32. If NTV were not exogenous over this period, it would not have risen in the way shown. This is also likely in that a major constituent of NTV is the rate of corporation tax, which is decided by governments and is therefore exogenous. This might be offset by other changes so that NTV in aggregate would be endogenous. But the tax rate has improved (i.e. fallen) over the period and, as Figure 32 shows, so has NTV, which thus also appears to be exogenous in aggregate.

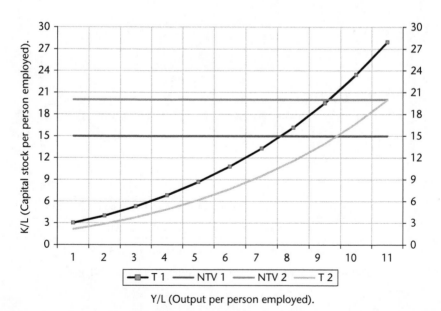

Figure 31. Output changes with TFP and NTV

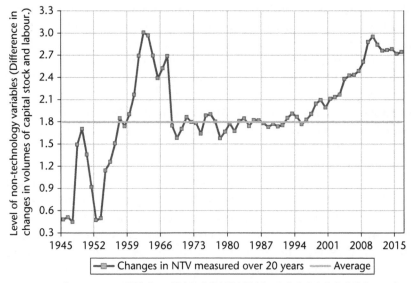

Data sources: BEA Asset Table 1.9 NIPA Tables 1.1.4, 1.1.5 & 3.9.5 + early
data from Bureau of the Census.

Figure 32. US: NTV is exogenous

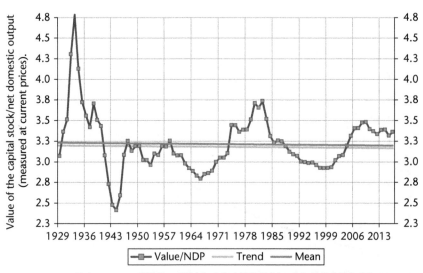

Data sources: BEA Asset Table 1.1, NIPA Tables 1.1.5, 3.9.5 & 5.1.

Figure 33. US: Mean reversion of capital stock value/NDP

While NTV is exogenous and the volume of the capital stock has risen relative to output, it is important to note that the value of the capital stock is mean-reverting. This can be shown in theory[3] and when tested is confirmed by the data which I illustrate in Figure 33.[4]

The value of the capital stock changes with expectations of future returns; however, these do not vary as much as output, so the value of the capital stock under conditions of full employment and assuming no errors in expectations has a constant ratio to output, as shown in Figure 33.

[3] While NTV is exogenous, the ratio of capital value to output is mean-reverting. Value (V) equals profits (Π) after tax at some multiple (θ) of the non-technology variables: e.g. a fall in the hurdle rate on equity will have increased the value of profits proportionately to the fall. Thus $V = \Pi \times \theta NTV$. Profits are the share of output which can be financed at the current level of NTV and are thus the level of output divided by some multiple (ε) of NTV: e.g. a fall in the hurdle rate will increase the level of profits proportionate to the fall. So $\Pi = Y/(\varepsilon NTV)$. Thus $V = (Y(/\varepsilon NTV)) \times (\theta NTV) = (\theta/\varepsilon) \times (Y)$.

[4] The mean reversion of the ratio between the value of the capital stock and output is shown by the closeness of the trend and mean.

11

The Results of My Model

All growth comes from changes in NTV, the volume of labour, and technology (TFP). TFP therefore represents the contribution to growth that does not come from changes in NTV and labour. As the model seeks to measure TFP under conditions of full employment, this needs to be over periods long enough for cyclical changes to have little impact. If the necessary data were available the model could be used to calculate changes in TFP for the US economy as a whole or for the corporate sector in isolation.

For the economy as a whole Figure 34 measures TFP over thirty years and Figure 35 over twenty. Both show that the growth of TFP has been on a long-term declining trend and over the most recent thirty and twenty-year

Data sources: BEA Asset Table 1.9, NIPA Tables 1.1.5, 1.1.6, 1.14 and 3.9.5. BLS Table LNS 11,000,000 and Z1 B. 103.

Figure 34. US: TFP measured over previous 30 years

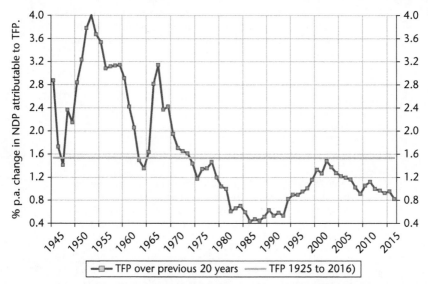

Data sources: BEA Asset Table 1.9, NIPA Tables 1.1.5, 1.1.6, 1.14 and 3.9.5.
BLS Table LNS 11,000,000 and Z1 B. 103.

Figure 35. US: TFP measured over previous 20 years

periods has been 0.9 per cent per annum and 0.8 per cent per annum respectively. Since 1980 TFP has fluctuated around these levels without any clear trend.

The Congressional Budget Office (CBO) uses estimates of TFP for its economic forecasts, and these seem a suitable basis for comparing the results derived from the model proposed in this book with those derived from the current consensus approach.

Table 7 compares the results for the specific periods chosen by the CBO.[1] While the model agrees with the CBO figures from 1981 to 1996 there are substantial differences thereafter. The model's figures for TFP are significantly lower than those used by the CBO, and the recovery in TFP shown in both when comparing the periods 1997 to 2005 and 1981 to 1996 is small according to the model and sharp according to the CBO.

One of the problems with the consensus model is that its use by different people produces different results.[2] I therefore compare in Table 8 other estimates for the specific periods chosen by the authors of a well-known paper.[3] Only for the period 1973 to 1995 are the results similar, and the differences are not only of quantity but in the direction of the changes. For example the model shows a decline in TFP comparing 1995 to 2004 with 1973 to 1995, whereas Byrne et al. show a strong rise.

---

[1] Shackleton (2018), Appendix C.   [2] Ghosh and Kraay (2000).
[3] Byrne, Fernald and Reinsdorf (2016).

Table 7. TFP (percentage change per annum), comparing the CBO's estimates with those derived from the model set out in this book (Data sources: CBO Working paper 2018–03 & as shown in Figure 35)

	Model	CBO
1981 to 1996	1.21	1.2
1997 to 2005	1.31	2.0
2006 to 2016	0.48	0.7

Table 8. TFP (percentage change per annum), comparing the estimates by Byrne, Fernald, and Reinsdorf (2016) with those derived from the model set out in this book (Data sources: Byrne, Fernald, and Reinsdorf (2016) and as shown in Figure 35)

	Model	Byrne et al.
1947 to 1973	2.62	2.10
1973 to 1995	0.58	0.52
1995 to 2004	−0.62	1.99
2004 to 2015	0.47	0.45

Changes in NTV reflect the different growth rates of the volumes of capital and labour and the impact these changes have on output, which varies over time with changes in the ratio of capital volume to output. Dividing the changes in NTV by the capital output ratio for the same period gives the impact of NTV on growth, and after deducting the change in the volume of labour we have the impact of TFP on labour productivity. Figure 36 measures this over the past twenty years, and shows that the contribution has fallen from nearly 100 per cent in the early post-war years to 60 per cent in 2016. The contribution to improved labour productivity through the increase in the capital stock resulting from favourable changes in NTV has thus been 40 per cent over the past twenty years. This shows that in the past, growth has been enhanced to a very large extent by changes in NTV; it follows that if these changes can be effected by policy then we can use policy to enhance growth, and are not solely at the mercy of changes in technology.

The results for TFP shown by the proposed model are very different from the consensus figures as shown in the examples, but this is partly a matter of which bit of the economy is being measured. The CBO and other consensus figures are for the non-farm business sector and define the volume of labour as total hours worked, while the data I have used on capital volume are for the whole economy.

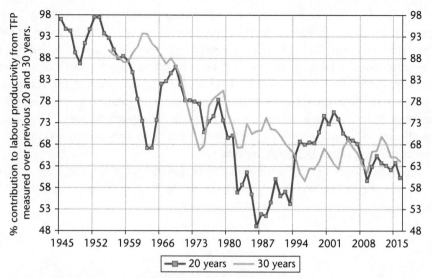

Data sources: BEA Asset Table 1.9, NIPA Tables 1.1.5, 1.1.6, 1.14 and 3.9.5.
BLS Table LNS 11,000,000 and Z1 B. 103.

Figure 36. US: Contribution to labour productivity from TFP

Table 9. TFP (percentage change per annum), comparing the CBO's estimates with those derived from the model set out in this book (Data sources: CBO Working paper 2018–03 & as shown in Figure 35)

	Model	CBO
1981 to 1996	1.21	0.9
1997 to 2005	1.31	1.5
2006 to 2016	0.48	0.525

Table 10. TFP (percentage change per annum), comparing the estimates by Byrne, Fernald, and Reinsdorf (2016) with those derived from the model set out in this book, allowing for difference in total economy and non-farm business sector (Data sources: Byrne, Fernald, and Reinsdorf (2016) and as shown in Figure 35)

	Model	Byrne et al.
1947 to 1973	2.62	1.58
1973 to 1995	0.58	0.39
1995 to 2004	−0.62	1.49
2004 to 2015	0.47	0.34

In order to compare my results based on data for the whole economy with those for the non-farm business sector, some assumptions need to be made on the extent to which TFP affects those parts of the economy excluded from the consensus measures. As the non-farm business sector constitutes three quarters of the total economy, the effect is in any case limited. If, for example, it is assumed that there has been no improvement in total factor productivity in the remaining quarter of the US economy, the comparisons are still marked, as shown in Tables 9 and 10, both with regard to the quantities and the directions of change between periods.

The differences between the consensus model and mine are large and a choice between the two thus needs to be made to determine the appropriate policy.

12

Testing the Proposed Model

Changes in NTV can be calculated from the differences between the growth rates of employment and of the volume of capital, and can also be calculated independently from the changes in the constituents of NTV. Given adequate data, the independence of these two approaches allows the model to be tested.[1]

The constituents of NTV are all measurable with respect to corporate output, though in the case of the hurdle rate only over the long-term. We can, however, test whether the hurdle rate is stable in the short run through the relationship between investment and changes in the return on corporate equity (net worth), which responds to changes in all the other constituents of NTV.

If we had data on corporate employment or if all national output was from corporations, the model could be tested by comparing changes in NTV calculated from changes in employment and the volume of capital, with changes in NTV calculated from data on the constituents of NTV and the return on corporate equity (RoE). In practice, due to limitations in the available data, we can only test the model by comparing the changes in NTV that apply to non-financial companies with those for NTV as calculated for the economy as a whole. The results are set out in Table 11. It shows the results of testing the changes in the constituents of NTV, derived from the data available for them, against changes in the value of NTV derived from the difference in the growth rates of the volumes of labour and capital.

The model seeks to calculate TFP via NTV on the basis of an economy operating at full employment. This requires that changes are measured over time periods long enough to reduce the impact of cyclical fluctuations in the economy. Longer time periods minimize their effect, but also reduce the information about recent trends. I have taken twenty years as providing a

---

[1] Formulae for the two measures of NTV are set out in Appendix 4, which shows inter alia that the two are drawn from totally independent sets of data.

Table 11. Measured over previous twenty years, R^2 correlations between changes in return on equity and the other constituents of NTV for non-financial US companies with changes in NTV as calculated for the economy as a whole from the difference in the growth of the volume of capital and employment (Data sources: BEA Asset Table 1.9, NIPA Tables 1.1.5, 1.14, 3.9.5, and 5.1, and Z1 Tables F.103 and B. 103)

Period	20-year periods from 1946 to 2016	20-year periods from 1966 to 2016
Profit margins	0.45	0.70
Net interest	0.31	0.08
Leverage (net debt as percentage of debt + net worth)	0.43	0.78
Tax rate	0.25	0.76
Return on equity (profits after tax without IV & CC as percentage of domestic net worth at historic cost)	0.16	0.54

reasonable balance. As the data needed for the calculations are only available since 1946, the first period for which the tests can be applied is for the twenty years from 1946 to 1966.

Figure 35 shows, however, that NTV was volatile for the earlier periods. This is presumably due to the difficulty of measuring NTV free from cyclical fluctuations in the early post-war years. I therefore show in Table 11 the correlations over all the available twenty-year periods covering the years 1946 to 2016, with those for the more recent twenty-year periods covering the years 1966 to 2016.

I illustrate the correlations between changes in NTV with those in profit margins and leverage in Figure 37 and for changes in tax and RoE in Figure 38. These show the way in which correlations have become stronger for periods after 1960 to 1980. Figure 38 also shows the strong R^2 correlations between the effective rate of corporation tax and RoE which has varied over the whole period 1946 to 2016 between 0.78 and 0.91.

As the changes in the constituents of NTV are derived independently from the changes in NTV in aggregate, significant correlations between the two are evidence for the robustness of the model and thus for the validity of the conclusions derived from it. Over the second period the cyclical fluctuations in the economy were relatively limited and the results should thus reflect the changes in NTV for an economy operating at full employment.

As Table 11 shows, the correlations are strong for profit margins and leverage throughout the whole period from 1946 to 2016 and for the period 1966 to 2016 are strong for all constituents of NTV except interest rates. The proposed model should therefore be preferred to the current consensus model. It is testable and robust when tested, while the standard approach appears to be untestable.

The evidence also suggests that the underlying assumptions of the consensus approach are not valid. As Figure 28 illustrates, companies do not take note

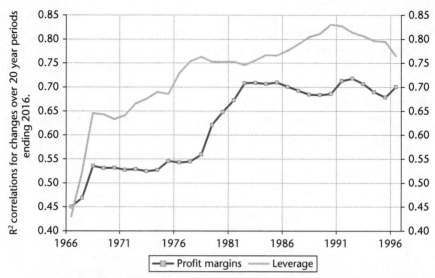

Data sources: BEA Asset Table 1.9, NIPA Tables 1.1.5, 1.1.6, 1.14 and 3.9.5.
BLS Table LNS 11,000,000 and Z1 B. 103.

Figure 37. US: Correlations between NTV, profit margins, and leverage

Data sources: BEA Asset Table 1.9, NIPA Tables 1.1.5, 1.1.6, 1.14 and 3.9.5.
BLS Table LNS 11,000,000 and Z1 B. 103.

Figure 38. US: Correlations between effective rate of corporation tax and RoEs

of changes in the cost of equity, and thus of capital, when deciding on their level of investment. The assumption that they should rests on the belief that it would be in the interests of shareholders for companies to increase the value of their capital stock by raising equity and making additional investment whenever the return was greater than the cost. Shareholders are, however, concerned with their wealth, which depends on share prices rather than the underlying value of the capital stock, and therefore object to the raising of equity as this tends to depress share prices.

13

Investment, the Capital Stock, and Economic Policy

We have data for the returns on equity (RoEs) of US non-financial companies, whose output constitutes around 50 per cent of GDP and are thus a smaller sample than the non-farm business sector. The definition of capital is also different, both because it is measured at value rather than by volume and because it includes non-produced assets, such as land and trade credit. RoE is measured by profits after tax as a percentage of corporate net worth and both these factors come in two forms. Profits are measured (NIPA Table 1.14) both with and without the inventory and capital consumption adjustments, which are designed to offset the impact of inflation, and assets are measured (Z1 Table B. 103) at both book values and at 'replacement cost', which also seeks to allow for inflation.

The data available to companies are based on their own balance sheets and profit and loss accounts, neither of which is adjusted for inflation. As company managements can only respond to data which they have, in Figure 39 I use profits and asset values which are similar to those given in corporate accounts and make no adjustment for inflation.

When the capital stock grows at the same rate as employment all growth in output is due to TFP. For growth to be faster there needs to be a beneficial change in NTV. If the constituents of NTV improve (with the exception of the hurdle rate on equity) there will be a rise in RoE and, if the hurdle rate on equity is unchanged, investment will rise. Since the hurdle rate is stable over the long-term, as can be seen from Figure 29, corporate investment should usually respond to changes in RoE and, as Figure 39 shows, it does.

The rise in the hurdle rate has therefore depressed investment and thus stifled the growth of the capital stock. This connection is not only inherently likely it is also what must happen. The capital stock can only grow in volume if investment exceeds the rate of scrapping and in value if it exceeds the rate of capital consumption. A rise in investment, as a result of a fall in the

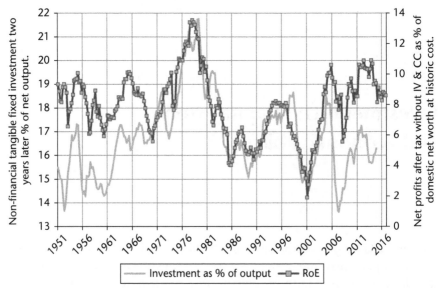

Data sources: Z1 Tables B. 103 & F. 103 and NIPA Tables 1.1.5 & 1.14.

Figure 39. US: Corporate investment and RoEs

hurdle rate, will increase both the volume and value of the capital stock unless it is matched by a rise in the rates of scrapping and capital consumption. In the absence of changes in its other constituents NTV must improve when the hurdle rate falls, and this raises the value of the capital stock. A fall in the hurdle rate in isolation will therefore increase both investment and the value of the capital stock, so the resulting rise in investment cannot be matched by a rise in capital consumption. The additional investment will also increase the volume of the capital stock as it will not be accompanied by any increase in the volume of labour, so the resulting rise in investment cannot be matched by a rise in scrapping. Increased investment due to a fall in the hurdle rate will therefore add to both the volume and the value of the capital stock. The rise in the hurdle rate indicated by the stability of the other constituents of NTV (Table 14) and the change in the relationship with RoE shown in Figure 39 would therefore, if reversed, cause a rise in investment and faster growth in both the value and the volume of the capital stock.

When the capital stock grows faster than employment, labour productivity rises by more than it would if changes in technology were the sole determinant of the change in output. Since NTV is not endogenous and its changes can stimulate growth, the model thus indicates the policy measures that could be taken to encourage improvements.

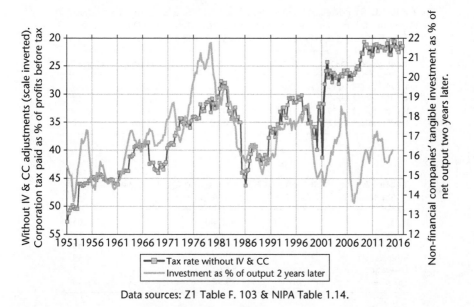

Data sources: Z1 Table F. 103 & NIPA Table 1.14.

Figure 40. US: Non-financial companies' investment and effective corporation tax rate

Table 12. R^2 correlations between US non-financial companies' tangible investment and their RoEs (Data sources: Z1 Tables F.103 and B.103 and NIPA Tables 1.1.5 and 1.14)

Timing of investment	Coincident	1 year later	2 years later	3 years later
Q4 1951 to Q3 2017	0.05	0.24	0.27	0.19
Q4 1951 to Q4 1999	0.12	0.3	0.31	0.29
Q1 1972 to Q4 1999	0.35	0.65	0.73	0.74
Q4 2000 to Q3 2017	0.01	0.14	0.25	0.01

Of the constituents of NTV, profit margins are high and not readily subject to change from policy moves, interest rates appear to have only at best a weak impact and are determined by other policy requirements, and leverage is already high, perhaps dangerously so. Changes in corporation tax and the hurdle rate thus seem to be the only credible options open if policy changes are to boost labour productivity.

Figure 40 shows that historically the effective rate of corporation tax has been strongly linked to the level of corporate tangible investment. Unfortunately it also shows that this relationship broke down after 2000, in a similar way to the change shown in Figure 39. The change in correlations over time is shown in Tables 12 and 13. The sharp change in the investment response to favourable changes in tax and RoEs must have occurred because of an adverse

Table 13. R^2 correlations between US non-financial companies' tangible investment and the effective rate of corporation tax (Data sources: Z1 Tables F.103 and B.103 and NIPA Tables 1.1.5 & 1.14)

Timing of investment	Coincident	1 year later	2 years later	3 years later
Q4 1951 to Q3 2017	0.05	0.06	0.07	0.06
Q4 1951 to Q4 1999	0.57	0.61	0.60	0.49
Q1 1972 to Q4 1999	0.33	0.41	0.43	0.33
Q4 2000 to Q3 2017	0.27[1]	0.05	0.06	0.11

Table 14. The constituents of NTV comparing Q4 2000 with Q4 2017 (Data sources: Z1 Table B. 103 and NIPA Table 1.14)[2]

	Q4 2000	Q4 2017
Profit margins	15.82	22.84
Interest rates	5.67	4.58
Leverage	84.67	89.73
Tax rate	39.92	21.48

change in one or more of the other constituents of NTV. However, as Table 14 shows, all these constituents have changed in a favourable direction except the hurdle rate on equity, which cannot be measured in the short term.

If is therefore clear that a rise in the hurdle rate of equity must be the cause of the current low level of tangible investment. As policy appears unable to affect TFP, an improvement in labour productivity (which today seems badly needed) requires steps to rein back the rise in the equity hurdle rate.

---

[1] The relationship was actually perverse; on a coincident basis investment increased as the tax rate rose.

[2] Profit margins are profits after capital consumption, but before interest and tax, as a percentage of output net of capital consumption; interest rates are net interest paid as a percentage of net interest-bearing liabilities; leverage is net interest-bearing assets as a percentage of net output; and the tax rate is tax paid as a percentage of profits before tax without IV & CC.

14

The Bonus Culture Has Raised the Hurdle Rate

The rise in the hurdle rate on equity represents a change in management behaviour and is readily explicable in terms of the preceding change in incentives. As Figure 41 shows, the average remuneration of US CEOs increased sharply from 1992 to 2000, accompanied by a sharp rise in the non-salary proportion. There have been no significant changes in either the total remuneration or the bonus proportion since 2000. This change in incentives had the usual effect, with a natural time lag, of changing behaviour. The benefits for management that come from improving short-term profits have risen sharply compared with the longer-term benefits from corporate investment, which are unchanged. This has had the effect of discouraging investment in a similar way as would a rise in the hurdle rate on equity.[1]

Without policy changes to offset this sharp change in management behaviour it will be difficult to increase the level of investment in the US significantly. In the absence of such an increase, it is unlikely that there will be an improvement in the trend rate at which labour productivity and output can grow.

The evidence shows that the dramatic and worrying fall in productivity is the result of low investment, caused by the equally dramatic change in the way corporate executives are paid. But such evidence is dry and can be unconvincing unless we understand the way in which the bonus culture has led to the fall in investment.

Companies last for much longer than the terms of office that CEOs expect or usually experience. The risks run by companies therefore have a much longer time horizon than those of their leaders. Possibly the greatest single risk for companies is losing market share. This risk is reduced by competitive pricing and investment in new equipment. The two are related. High levels of investment reduce the risk that other companies will, by investing more, have lower

---

[1] For a detailed explanation see Smithers (2016).

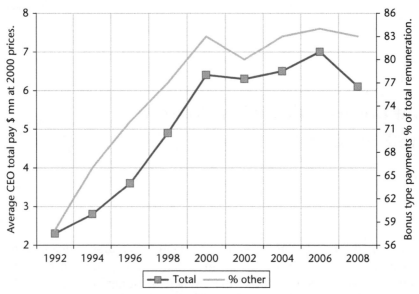

Data source: Carola Frydman & Dirk Jenter NBER Working Paper 16585.

Figure 41. US: Change in management incentives

production costs and will therefore be in a position to price their output more competitively. This is because new equipment has embodied in it more up-to-date technology than older plant, and therefore has lower costs of production. The key concern for management is optimizing the metrics that determine their pay. The greater the bonus element in managers' remuneration, the greater will be their attention to those metrics and the less they will be concerned about the longer-term risks incurred by the companies they manage.

Most companies, with the marked exception of producers of oil and other raw materials, have considerable short-term monopoly power as their customers cannot usually switch to another supplier without considerable difficulty. However, it is not in a company's longer-term interests to exploit this monopoly power, because the more it does so the greater will be the risk that its customers will seek out alternative sources of supply. The longer-term interests of the company in preserving its market share are thus at odds with the wish to maximize short-term profits. Modern management incentive plans increase the reward for taking the short-term benefit from aggressive pricing, but at the cost of increasing the long-term risk that customers will switch to other suppliers. We should therefore expect the change in management remuneration to push up profit margins.

Since modern remuneration plans are now common to many companies, the incentive to exploit monopoly power more aggressively is widespread, adding to the difficulty faced by each company's customers in obtaining alternative supplies at lower prices. The impact of incentives on pushing up profit margins is thus further increased, and, as Figure 42 shows, profit margins are indeed currently above average.[2]

Companies generate cash from their profits and depreciation allowances and can raise additional funds through issues of debt or equity. In addition to the need to fund working capital, they can use cash in three basic ways. They can invest in new capital equipment, they can pay dividends, or they can buy back shares. The latest and most efficient technology is found in new equipment, so the more a company invests the higher will be the proportion of its equipment which is up-to-date and most efficient. Tangible capital investment thus lowers a company's long-term production costs and thereby reduces the risk that it will lose market share to more efficient competitors. Those competitors can be at least equally profitable while undercutting companies which have invested less, by setting lower prices or by outspending

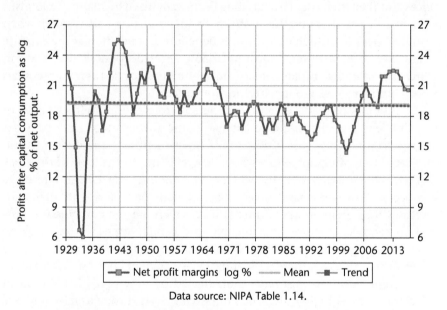

Data source: NIPA Table 1.14.

Figure 42. US: Non-financial profit margins, annual 1929 to 2017

[2] The closeness of the trend and the average shown in Figure 42 is an indication that profit margins are mean-reverting. See Appendix 5 for the theoretical explanation. It is because margins are mean-reverting that it is possible to say that they are currently above average.

them on advertising and other marketing expenditure. However, capital investment has the disadvantage that the short-term impact on profits is usually negative, as costs are incurred before the benefits arise. In addition, money spent on equipment cannot also be used for dividends and buy-backs. Capital investment therefore reduces the ability of management to boost its remuneration.

Over the long-term, investment must have given the same returns on equity to corporations as those received by shareholders. The long-term return on corporate equity has averaged around 6 per cent in real terms, which is well above the current cost of equity capital. When, as today, the US stock market is 70 per cent overvalued, this is around 3.5 per cent. Those with savings to invest would therefore like managements to increase their level of capital spending, as this should provide a 6 per cent long-term real return, whereas dividends reinvested in the stock market, at its current high level, will give a long-term return of only 3.5 per cent. There is, therefore, a difference between the interests of the retired, who wish to spend some of their accumulated capital as well as the dividends they receive from their shareholdings, and those who are saving for their retirement. The former benefit from high share prices and the latter lose. This has long been recognized by many economists, who have written about the problem of intergenerational inequity when sustained periods of high or low prices benefit one generation at the expense of another. It is, however, almost invariably ignored in public discussion in which 'the interests of shareholders' are habitually discussed as if shareholders were a homogeneous group with the same interests.

The interests of management are different from those of either savers or shareholders, and the dramatic change in the way managers are paid has hugely magnified the gap. It now pays management to prefer dividends and buy-backs to new equipment, without any reference to the level of the stock market. Share prices tend to rise when companies increase dividends or make buy-backs. Provided share prices don't actually fall, a rise in dividends increases total shareholder returns (TSRs), which are the combined returns that shareholders receive from income and capital appreciation. Investors place their main emphasis when valuing shares on the ratio between share prices and earnings per share (EPS) and to a lesser extent on the dividend yield. The current price/earnings ratio is unaffected by how much is paid out in dividends, and as higher dividends improve the yield they usually improve share prices. Buy-backs can be even more effective than dividends in raising TSRs. At the current level of the stock market, as I show in Table 15, borrowing money to buy back shares raises EPS for quoted companies, provided they can borrow at less than 6.7 per cent. This will fall in 2018, if pre-tax profits are unchanged, to 5.5 per cent, but will still be above the current cost of debt for most companies today.

Table 15. Break-even cost of interest, before tax, required to increase EPS on the S&P 500 as at 31 December 2017 (Data source: Standard & Poor's)

	2017 Tax	2018 Tax
S&P 500 31st December 2017 (A)	2673.61	2673.61
EPS for year to 31st December 2017 (B)	109.88	109.88
Earnings' yield (C) = (B) × 100 ÷ (A)	4.11	4.11
Assumed marginal rate of corporation tax (Federal rate + 4 per cent average state tax (D))	39 per cent	25 per cent
Break-even cost of debt before tax (E) = (C) ÷ (100−D)	6.7	5.5

Buy-backs tend to raise share prices, and thus also TSRs, not only because this is the usual impact on the market when additional buyers appear, but also because at current interest rates the reduction in profits resulting from the additional interest paid is less than the reduction in the number of shares. TSRs are a common metric used for measuring the success of management, but they are not the only one. Buy-backs will also improve other metrics such as RoE and EPS.

Companies can increase their EPS not only by buying their own shares but by buying other companies through mergers and acquisitions. As they usually have to pay a premium over the current share price when making takeovers, the break-even level of interest rates would be lower than that for buy-backs, unless the merger of the two companies allowed their combined costs to be cut. This is usually claimed by the buyers, although these hopes are not necessarily realized.

The short-term impact on EPS from investing in new plant and equipment is usually negative, because the costs involved are immediate and there is usually a delay before the rewards from lower costs arrive, while money spent on buy-backs and takeovers is usually positive in the short-term. It is therefore not surprising that, at current levels of interest rates and so long as interest is a deductible cost for corporation tax, managements who are paid to raise EPS will prefer share buying to capital investment.

The change in management incentives has been accompanied by a behavioural change that favours distributing cash to shareholders through buy-backs and dividends. Figure 43 illustrates this change. The proportion of cash flow distributed to shareholders has more than doubled since the late 1990s, while that spent on equipment has fallen.

The year 2000 shows up in Figures 39 and 40 as a turning point when investment ceased to respond to the levels of corporation tax and RoE. As Table 16 shows, it also marked the start of a sharp change in the use of corporate cash. These changes followed the sharp rise in incentives shown in Figure 42 and are its expected result, which suggests that it is therefore the probable cause.

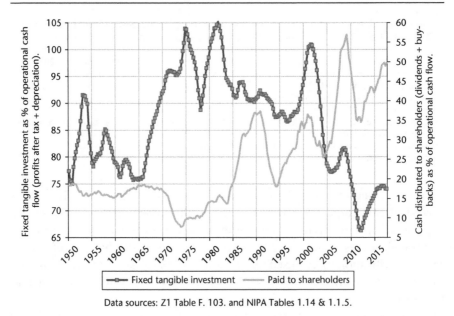

Data sources: Z1 Table F. 103. and NIPA Tables 1.14 & 1.1.5.

Figure 43. US: Non-financial companies' cash invested and distributed to shareholders

Table 16. Percentage of US non-financial companies' cash from operations invested and percentage distributed in cash to shareholders (Data source: Federal Reserve: Z1 Table F. 103)

	Fixed tangible investment	Paid to shareholders
1947 to 1999	88.96	19.56
2000 to 2017	77.80	40.70

These perverse incentives are likely to have a stronger impact on quoted than on unquoted companies. The latter include foreign-owned companies with different cultures and incentive structures and US-owned ones whose managements have significant ownership stakes and who thus take a longer view of their companies' interests. Research shows that quoted and unquoted companies are in aggregate of similar importance in the economy but that in recent years unquoted companies have been investing twice as much as quoted ones. This provides additional evidence of the bad impact on the economy that has been caused by modern management pay systems. The authors of the research investigated whether short-termism distorts the investment decisions of stock market listed firms: 'Our results show that compared with private (i.e. unquoted) firms, public firms (i.e. quoted) invest substantially less. These findings are consistent with the notion that short-termist pressures distort investment decisions.'[3]

The evidence that the decline in productivity has been induced by weak investment by large companies is also found in the UK. This was pointed out in an article headed 'UK's biggest companies are productivity slackers',[4] which cited the finding of a new research paper that a low level of investment (termed 'capital shallowing') 'has become increasingly important in explaining the labour productivity growth gap in service sectors, as the buoyancy of the UK labour market has not been sufficiently matched by investment'.[5]

In addition to this evidence there is strong theoretical support for the damage done by the incentives of the bonus culture. A paper by Roland Bénabou and Nobel Laureate Jean Tirole provides a theoretic framework to show that the bonus culture increases inequality and lowers investment, work ethics and welfare.[6] In a paper originally prepared for the Federal Reserve Bank of New York its authors remark that bonus incentives encourage managers to reduce their firms' equity to the minimum level possible.[7]

---

[3] See Asker, Farre-Mensa and Ljungqvist (2015). I have been unable to find data for the UK, but it seems likely that if available they would show a similar pattern.

[4] Giles (2018).   [5] Riley, Rincon-Aznar and Samek (2018).

[6] Bénabou and Tirole (2016).

[7] This is my paraphrase to avoid the technical terms used. In the authors' words, 'this means that convex contracts may induce the self-interested manager to adopt investment policies that drive his firm's equilibrium capital stock to zero': Donaldson, Gershun and Giannoni (2011).

15

The Added Impact of Misinformation

Growth has suffered from a rise in hurdle rates. While the change in the incentives for management resulting from the bonus culture seems to have been the key cause, it has probably been amplified by very high and misleading assumptions commonly made about the cost of equity capital.

As I illustrated in Figure 26, the real return to shareholders has rotated around 6 per cent per annum, and with the US stock market being currently at least 70 per cent overpriced, as Figure 27 shows, the cost of equity capital should be around 3.5 per cent real (i.e. 6 per cent divided by 1.7).[1] It is nonetheless common to encounter estimates of the cost of equity capital today for individual companies which are multiples of this. The cost for individual companies can vary around this average but must equal it in aggregate. We can therefore be sure that the commonly published figures for the cost of equity are nonsense; unfortunately they are also damaging nonsense.

When estimating the cost of equity capital we need to make a distinction between financial and non-financial companies. The latter's assets are a combination of real and financial ones, but they also have financial liabilities which offset their financial assets. To achieve a real return of 6 per cent they only need a current return on equity (RoE) of 6 per cent, as the impact of inflation will be to raise the value of their real assets proportionately. In the case of banks and other financial companies the bulk of their net worth is represented by financial assets, and to allow for inflation they will need to have a current RoE higher than that needed for non-financials.

KPMG, one of the top ranked firms of Chartered Accountants, recently claimed that Britain's five largest banking groups must 'urgently tackle' low returns for shareholders, because none of the banks were currently achieving a

---

[1] This does not mean that this will be the return to investors, which will vary with how long the investment is held, whether dividends are reinvested, and, if so, the level of the market when the reinvestment takes place.

return on equity above 8 per cent.[2] Another example comes from the Boston Consulting Group, according to whom 'investment banks' cost of capital is typically estimated at about 10 per cent'.[3] Allowing for 2 per cent inflation this represents a real return of 8 per cent, which is well above the long-term real return on equity. Similarly KPMG's scorned 8 per cent is around the historic average (allowing for 2 per cent inflation). Estimates for the cost of capital that are well above past returns on capital seem to be general. In a speech in 2016 Martin Taylor, a member of the Bank of England's Financial Policy Committee, remarked: 'If banks seek unsustainably high returns, whether as a result of a genuine market constraint or an imagined hurdle, they can do a lot of damage to the rest of us … last year [2015] the major UK banks were mostly publishing medium-term targets for return on equity of between 10 and 13 per cent, with some target ranges stretching as high as 15 per cent.'[4] Absurd estimates of the cost of equity and thus of hurdle rates are usual for non-financial as well as financial companies—and for non-financial companies there is no need to add any allowance for the impact of inflation. The FT's Lex column has quoted a cost of capital of 9–10 per cent for BT's Openreach division.[5]

Chief executives tend to believe what they read, at least when the source appears to be authoritative. If they are persistently misinformed that the cost of equity is much higher than 6 per cent, they will turn down investment opportunities where the expected return exceeds the long-term hurdle rate, let alone the real cost of equity capital. One reason why the cost of equity capital is so egregiously overestimated by accountants and others in the financial services industry is that claims made by companies about their historic returns are greatly overstated. For example the RoEs published by non-financial companies listed in the S&P 500 Index for the year to 31 March 2014 averaged 17 per cent per annum.[6] As Figure 31 shows, this was a year in which profit margins were at their average level, and we should therefore expect profitability to be around long-term average levels. However, if the published figures were correct then RoEs would currently be nearly three times their historic average level.

RoEs are clearly overstated, and there are a variety of reasons how this comes about. An important one is that assets are shown in balance sheets at book values, which represent the original cost minus depreciation. Inflation will usually have raised current value well above these book values, even after allowing for depreciation, and so at today's costs corporate net worth is higher than book value. The situation is complicated because published profits are habitually overstated,[7] and (as dividends are known accurately) this means

---

[2] Dunkley (2015).   [3] Noonan (2016).   [4] Taylor (2016).
[5] *Financial Times*, 20 July 2016.   [6] For details see Appendix 5.   [7] See Appendix 6.

that retained profits are proportionately overstated even more.[8] Net worth is largely the sum of past retained profits and is thus overstated to the same degree.

We can, however, isolate the impact of inflation on RoEs[9] from US national accounting data which are available using balance sheets based on both current and historic (book value) prices. I show the way that these returns have varied in Figure 44, which compares those measured at book values (at historic cost) with those allowing for inflation (calculated using the current cost of assets). As Figure 44 shows, the returns measured at historic cost have been persistently higher than those based on current cost.

In Table 17 I use the ratio between these two measures to estimate the impact of inflation. As national account profits are measured in two ways I show the impact using both measures. (Inflation affects profits through the impact on inventories (IV) and on capital consumption (CC).)

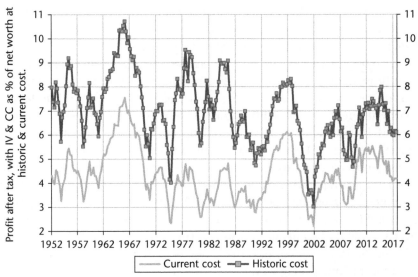

Data sources: Z1 Table B. 103, & NIPA Table 1.14.

Figure 44. US: Non-financial RoEs at current and historic cost

---

[8] For example, if profits after tax are overstated by 15 per cent and dividends equal 60 per cent of published profits then retained profits will be only 27 per cent of 'true' profits and thus 33 per cent below the apparent level.

[9] The RoEs are calculated on the basis of domestic profits and net worth data, which include the values of both direct inward and outward investment. This can be adjusted when using current cost data, but not for historic cost data as the direct investment figures are only available on a current cost basis. The result is to underestimate RoEs, but this should not affect the ratios between those measured at historic and current cost.

Table 17. Extent to which US RoEs were boosted in the 12 months to Q1 2014 by using historic cost values for assets (Data sources: Federal Reserve Z1 Table B 103 and NIPA Table 1.14)

RoEs with profits after tax with IV & CC		RoEs with profits after tax without IV & CC	
At historic cost (A)	7.02	At historic cost (E)	7.75
At current cost (B)	5.04	At current cost (F)	5.56
Ratio (C) = (A) ÷ (B)	1.39	Ratio (G) = (E) ÷ (F)	1.39
S&P 500 RoE (D)	17.00	S&P 500 RoE (D)	17.00
Adjusted (D) ÷ (C)	12.20	Adjusted (D) ÷ (F)	12.20

The bonus culture has given management a strong incentive to misrepresent the RoEs that their companies publish. Bonuses depend on changes in profits and share prices, compared to some previous level. In bad times it can therefore be in the interests of management to present abysmal profit figures, rather than merely bad ones. When things become so bad that management is changed, the new arrivals will want the level of profits when they take over to appear as low as possible, not only from a wish to blame their predecessors for the collapse but also to make subsequent profits look good. Even those managers who survive will wish to publish very bad profits in a poor year. They will then appear to have a strong case for scrapping the former profit targets and introducing new ones, in which success will be judged by the extent to which profits rise compared with their now heavily depressed level rather than with those published when things were going well. After a dramatic fall in profits, remuneration committees will think it only reasonable that bonus arrangements will not incentivise management if the profit targets appear to be out of reach. It thus seems sensible to reduce the level of profits which must be exceeded before future bonuses will become payable.

These arguments for scrapping previous targets are bogus, despite their proponents' assertions. Making write-offs in bad years not only depresses the base from which future changes are judged but also makes subsequent profit increases much easier. When write-offs take place the effect is to reduce the book value of companies' assets, such as their inventories, trade debtors and equipment. The lower the book values of inventories the greater will be the profits when they are subsequently sold, and the lower the book value of debts the greater will be the profits when payments are received from debtors. In the case of equipment, the lower its book value the lower will be the subsequent charge for depreciation—and again this will increase future profits. Write-offs are not just an admission that profits have been overstated in the past; they are also an implied promise that profits will be overstated in the future. This belongs to a rare group of management promises: those that are usually kept.

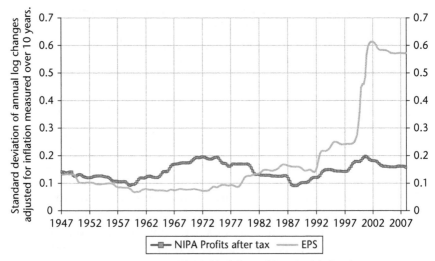

Data sources: NIPA Table 1.14 and Standard & Poor's.

Figure 45. US: Volatility of S&P 500 EPS and NIPA profits after tax

By exaggerating profit falls and their subsequent recoveries, the bonus culture encourages companies to publish profits which are much more volatile than before. This is exactly what has occurred. The increased volatility of published profits, which I illustrate in Figure 45, provides additional evidence of the impact of the change in management incentives on management behaviour. We have data for the US back to 1947, both for profits after tax shown in the national accounts and for earnings per share published for quoted companies in the S&P 500 Index. Figure 45 compares the volatility of these two series: they are very similar from 1947 to 2000, but in the twenty-first century the volatility of the published profits of quoted companies has become four times greater than the volatility of profits in the national accounts.

National data are inherently more accurate than those published by companies. A nation's gross output is measured by its GDP, and this can be calculated from both expenditure and income data. The two calculations must agree and, subject to small statistical discrepancies, they do. There are no similar checks on the accuracy of the data published by companies, but the rise in the relative volatility of their published data compared with those in the national accounts provides strong evidence that corporate data have become increasingly less accurate in recent years and that this deterioration has been encouraged by the change in management pay.

Companies with high RoEs are praised by analysts, and this is reflected in the reputations of their managements and directly or indirectly in their pay.

However, this encourages bad practice and poor outcomes. RoEs in Anglophone economies have begun to resemble tractors in communist Russia: just as targets for production encouraged the output of vast numbers of tractors which broke down, so targets for RoE serve to improve the published figures at the expense of a decline in the information they convey.

I showed in Table 17 that, even allowing for inflation, the published RoEs of US non-financial companies in 2014 were nearly twice their long-term average. As margins were then at their average level this is unlikely to be due to a historically high level of profits. It is therefore probable that, owing to the write-offs of assets in the 2008 recession, current asset prices were understated and current profits overstated by more than the usual extent. It is unlikely that this has changed much since, and it is also likely that the incentive to overstate profits is much greater for quoted companies than for others. Today the published profits of US quoted companies are therefore likely to be more than usually overstated.[10]

The massive increase in incentive payments, shown in Figure 41, was initially driven by calls for payment systems that aligned the interests of managements and shareholders more closely. The result has been to widen rather than close the gap. The initial result was for companies to offer share options to management; although this has become less fashionable, other approaches are very similar in their impact.[11] The famous Black–Scholes equation shows that the value of options depends on the volatility of the price of the shares to which they relate, rather than on the long-term returns on those shares. The effect of giving options to management thus has the effect of encouraging companies to increase the volatility of profits and of companies' share prices. Although the mechanism is slightly different, the bonus culture has had the same effect: I show the resulting volatility of profits in Figure 45. While pushing up share prices can be in the interests of short-term investors, increased volatility increases the risks to investors and is thus a disadvantage to longer-term holders.

We should expect the change in management incentives to encourage lower investment, higher profit margins, and a rise in the volatility of companies' published profits and for the level of investment by quoted companies to be lower than that of unquoted ones.[12] That these have indeed occurred is evidence that they are the result of the bonus culture.

The apparent paradox of high returns and low investment in the US has been given space by Paul Krugman in his *New York Times* articles. He puts forward the idea that this may be the result of a fall in competition,[13]

---

[10] Appendix 5 sets out the evidence that US profits are habitually overstated.
[11] In economic terms both are highly convex contracts.
[12] See Asker, Farre-Mensa and Ljungqvist (2015).   [13] Krugman (2016).

suggesting that today's high level of corporate profits represents not competitive returns on investment but growing monopoly power. The consequent high profits are available for managements to plunder for their own benefit through buy-backs. Management thus lacks a drive to increase profits by investment, which has consequently languished. A similar argument has been put forward by others.[14] Under my preferred explanation, the perverse incentives of the bonus culture cause managements to exploit the short-term monopoly power of their companies more strongly than before, with an impact similar in some respects to that of a fall in competition.

The claim that weak investment is explained by increasing concentration of business, with a consequent fall in competition, is shaky on several grounds. Concentration may have increased in the US, but I am aware of no claims that it has also risen in the UK, where investment by large companies has also been low.[15] Though concentration is assumed to indicate changes in monopoly power, many economists consider that ease of entry is a better indicator. For example, the sole ferry across a river would not be able to charge monopoly prices even if there were no other crossing, so long as it was easy to set up a competitive service. Even if we assume that competition falls with concentration, it is far from obvious that it will cause investment to fall. To establish that concentration has lowered investment since 2000 it is necessary either to show that the rise in concentration is a unique post-war experience or that past changes have affected investment. Neither of these has been claimed seriously (and there appear to be no data available for the necessary tests[16]), whereas the explanation that the bonus culture is responsible for the low level of investment is supported by long-term data set out in Figure 46, which show that the change in the way management is paid is a unique feature of the post-war world.

Figures 41 and 46 show that the huge change in US management remuneration took place from 1992 to 2000, after only slowly changing over the previous fifty-three years, and is thus consistent with the apparent change in corporate behaviour that occurred by 2000 as shown in Figures 39 and 40. The hypothesis that the lower than expected level of investment after 2000 is the result of the change in management remuneration is therefore supported by the evidence. Prior to 2000 there was no shortfall in the level of investment compared with expectations—neither those derived from tax data (Figure 40) nor from RoEs (Figure 39). Figure 46 shows that the rise in management bonuses in the run-up to 2000 shown in Figure 41 had no

---

[14] Döttling, Gutiérrez and Philippon (2017).   [15] Riley, Rincon-Aznar and Samek (2018).
[16] For example, those for the widely used Herfindahl–Hirschman index of business concentration do not seem to be available before 1997.

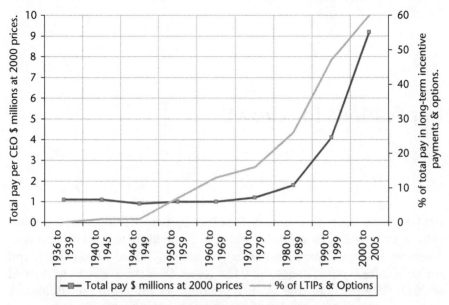

Data source: Carola Frydman & Dick Jenter NBER working paper 16585.

Figure 46: US: CEO pay 1936 to 2005

precedent in earlier years. The uniqueness of both events supports the hypothesis that they are causally related. The bonus culture also accounts—as increased monopoly does not—for the different levels of investment by quoted and unquoted companies[17] and for the increased volatility of published profits (Figure 45).

---

[17] Asker, Farre-Mensa and Ljungqvist (2015).

16

Implications for Growth

If no policy measures are introduced to offset the negative impact of the bonus culture, investment, productivity and growth are likely to remain depressed. The rates of improvement in labour productivity in the UK (Figure 2) and the US (Figure 3) have fallen to very low levels. Over the five years to the end of 2017, GDP per hour rose by 0.77 per cent per annum in the UK and by 0.57 per cent per annum in the US. If there are no changes in unemployment, hours worked per person and participation rates, the trend growth rate of the two economies will be the rate at which productivity improves plus the growth of the working age population, which over the next five years is expected to be 0.23 per cent per annum for the UK and 0.30 per cent per annum for the US. If there is no improvement in labour productivity the UK's trend growth rate will thus be 1 per cent and that of the US 0.87 per cent.

The data on the value and growth of the tangible capital stock provide another way to assess the trend growth rates of the US, though unfortunately we do not have data for the UK. In 2016 the US tangible capital stock grew by 1.1 per cent, which was also the average for the past five years. Figure 6 shows that the tangible capital/output ratio for the US was quite close to its average level: this provides another, slightly better indication of the likely trend growth rate of the US compared to those derived from the recent growth of productivity and the expected growth of the labour force.

The prospects for the UK and US are so poor that policy measures to stimulate growth are vital. All growth is the result of changes in either TFP or NTV, so one or other must improve to avoid stagnation.

Figures 34 and 35 show that there has been a long-term fall in US TFP. This has occurred despite a sharp rise in intangible investment, measured either as a proportion of total investment or of GDP. It appears that investment in R&D is either ineffective in boosting TFP or its level is badly measured. On either assumption, attempts to boost TFP through tax credits do not seem to work. TFP could probably be boosted by improving education and training, but any effect is likely to be very slow and very expensive. It follows that if growth is to be boosted within a reasonable time frame by policy changes, they need to be concentrated on improving NTV in aggregate and thus on one or more of its constituents. This is difficult. Nominal interest rates cannot fall any further, and it appears from macroeconomic analysis that investment does not respond to changes in real rates.[1] Corporate leverage is nearly back to its peak reached in 2009, which proved to be a very dangerous level (Figure 25).

Profit margins are mean-reverting and above average (Figure 42). They could rise further but are not readily amenable to widening through policy changes. The remaining constituents of NTV are corporation tax and the hurdle rate on equity, and, as Figures 39 and 40 show, corporate investment has ceased to respond to helpful changes in them since 2000. This appears to have been due to the perverse incentives of the bonus culture. Policy changes to restore a satisfactory rate of growth must therefore reverse this.

Fortunately there is considerable scope for investment—and hence growth—to recover should the damage from the bonus culture be ended. Figure 40 shows that corporate investment is 20 per cent below average, while the effective tax rate is at its lowest post-war level. Figure 39 also shows that investment is very low compared with the current level of RoE.

---

[1] Fair (2015). Also see Appendix 1.

17

Management and Shareholder Interests

The growth in management pay has received attention on the grounds that it is unfair, morally unpleasant, and has contributed to the growing inequality of incomes. These are serious issues in themselves, but they have unfortunately diverted attention from the economic damage done by the way in which management is paid. High pay has also been misinterpreted as being an issue only between management and shareholders. Because management has benefited so greatly, it is assumed that this has been at the expense of shareholders, and much energy has been expended on trying to persuade shareholders to change the way management is paid. This has been fruitless for two reasons. The most important is that it is the damage done to the economy rather than to shareholders which is the central issue.

The less important question is whether shareholders' interests have in fact been damaged. Shareholders are not a homogeneous group: those who have retired like high prices as they are naturally sellers of shares, but those who are saving for their retirement should like low prices so that they will have high returns on their savings. But it seems unlikely that many recognize their 'real interests' in this way—no group of shareholders likes, in practice, to have the prices of their shares decline. The impact of the bonus culture has thus been to benefit the retired at the expense of savers, but even the latter are not easily persuaded to call for lower share prices. Investors have a clear interest in low prices for the shares they don't own; but as the prices of different companies' shares move together, lower prices for the shares they don't own will usually be accompanied by lower prices for those they do. Issuing new shares or cutting dividends will usually reduce share prices, but shareholders have to own shares in companies before they can vote for such actions to be taken.

It is often assumed that shareholders in aggregate will benefit from faster growth in GDP, as this will produce higher equity returns. This assumption is, however, unjustified. Returns to shareholders do not rise and fall in response to changes in economic growth. Considered in total, shareholders of quoted companies do not appear to suffer in countries with lower economic growth because of low levels of investment. This can be seen by comparing the growth rates of different countries and the returns that have accrued to shareholders. It is generally acknowledged that returns to shareholders have not been higher for companies listed in countries with rapidly growing economies than for those listed in countries where growth has been slower.

We have data since 1899 for both the growth rates and the stock market returns for seventeen countries and, as I illustrate in Figure 47, there seems to be no relationship between the two for individual countries. For example, the UK has been the slowest growing economy among the seventeen, but has shown an above average return to shareholders, whereas Japan, which has been the second most rapidly growing economy, has had a well below average return. The lack of correlation between growth and stock market returns is not only what we observe: it is what we should expect. If fast growth were expected to produce higher returns to shareholders, then investors would shower capital into those economies which were expected to grow rapidly. High levels of investment should boost growth; but the efficiency of investment is also likely to fall as the amount increases, so that the greater the amount of investment the lower the return on each unit of investment is likely to be. If investors are correct in their expectations about growth, then the level of investment in rapidly growing economies is likely to be boosted to the point at which investor returns are the same, whatever the growth rate of the economy. Fast growth is a boon for workers, whose real wages rise faster in rapidly growing economies, but not for investors who should expect similar returns from all stock markets.

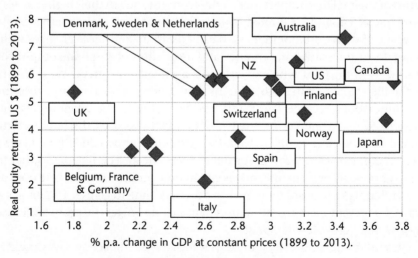

Figure 47. Growth and real equity returns

The change in management incentives has led to three major changes in companies' behaviour. They have higher profit margins, invest less and their published profits are more volatile. It is hard to argue that above average profit margins are contrary to the interests of shareholders. It certainly isn't in the short-term, though it might be in the longer-term if it led to quoted companies losing market share to unquoted and foreign-owned ones. The short-term rise in the profit margins of quoted companies would then be followed by a longer period during which their margins would be depressed relative to those of other companies. The same comments apply to low levels of investment, but only if one is considering quoted companies relative to all others.

The impact of management incentives on shareholder returns is thus not necessarily adverse. Margins will be boosted which, at least in the shorter term, is positive for shareholders. The lower level of investment is unlikely to hit shareholders' returns provided that it is common to all companies, and weak capital spending combined with high margins will not therefore necessarily lead to low returns on corporate capital. There is nonetheless a serious problem for investors in quoted companies, which seem to invest less than unquoted ones—a group that includes foreign-owned companies. It is likely, if this situation were to continue, that the longer-term disadvantages of low capital investment would become more important and those companies which are currently quoted would lose market share to foreign and domestically-owned unquoted companies.

If it became apparent that this were happening, investors would be likely to seek to divert their capital away from UK and US quoted companies towards foreign-owned and unquoted ones. Stock market values would then be likely to adjust to favour the second group. These would anyway be tending to rise in terms of their relative importance to the economy, due to their higher levels of investment. UK and US quoted companies would then be in relative decline in terms of both output and marked capitalization, and these changes would bring down the market importance and proportion of corporate output controlled by companies with perverse management incentives. With this fall the ability to maintain high margins would become weaker, and incentive schemes would become fewer and less damaging to the economy as their benefits to management declined. The problem posed by the bonus culture would not therefore be likely to last indefinitely, but would still be likely to remain a drawback to growth for many years ahead. The likelihood that the damage done by perverse incentives will in time produce its own cure does not mean that we can afford to allow the necessary time to elapse. The longer we leave the present incentive structures in place, the longer the problems caused by low trend growth will persist.

On a more cheering note, it looks as if the adverse impact on investment for UK and US quoted companies is becoming recognized, albeit slowly. One important sign is that it has become much easier for unquoted companies to raise new capital without the necessity of first becoming quoted and for the existing shareholders of unquoted companies to sell their holdings. However, it remains difficult for investors to shift their savings from being largely invested in quoted companies towards a greater exposure in unquoted ones. There is a huge difference between the ease with which investors shift their holdings from one quoted company to another and the difficulty of shifting a significant portion of their wealth from quoted to unquoted companies. This gap is the main reason why companies are quoted. Shareholders value the liquidity which quotation provides, not only because it enables them to shift their capital from one company to another but also because it allows them to change the distribution of their assets between cash, bonds and equities. The ability to make these shifts is not only prized because investors can adjust their portfolios to their changing views of the value and prospects for financial assets, but also because such changes are sensible for individual investors as they age, and thus also for pension funds with ageing beneficiaries.

Investment management falls into two main groups. Portfolios may be actively or passively managed. Success for the managers of actively managed funds is measured by comparing their performance with an index which seeks to show the returns that would have been achieved had the portfolio been the same as that of the average investor in a given stock market or asset class. For example, a fund investing in US equities would probably be compared with the S&P 500 Index. Passively managed portfolios simply seek to match the Index's performance. Those selling actively managed funds are unlikely to worry if the performance of the Index compares unfavourably with funds invested in unquoted companies, but the managers of passive 'tracker' funds should become concerned. We may therefore see them becoming worried about the long-term performance of quoted companies. I would be pleasantly surprised if this concern were to cause them to press quoted companies to reform their current management pay structures, but they should at least be one important group who would see advantages to their business if governments sought to change the bonus culture, and thus should be politically helpful if the debate on reform were to become less muted.

The damage done by the perverse incentives is to the economy rather than to shareholders. It will not therefore be addressed by appealing to shareholders; it must be addressed by governments acting in the interests of the general public.

18

Distractions from Serious Debate

Given the threat that we face it is important that we are not complacent about our current prospects or defeatist about our ability to change them. Robert Gordon is realistic and not complacent about our prospects, but I disagree strongly with his defeatism when he writes: 'There is little room for policy to boost investment, since years of easy monetary policy and high profits have provided more investment funds than firms have chosen to use.'[1] Firms don't make decisions, managers do; and they are choosing not to invest, not because their companies lack either the resources or profitable outlets for new investment, but because the perverse incentives of their pay packets make investment against their interests. The current low level of corporate investment is not caused by a lack of opportunities for profitable investment but by the bonus culture, and can therefore be cured if its incentives are reversed.

Despite Robert Gordon's eminence and his caution about our prospects, conventional wisdom remains complacent, as is shown by official forecasts which habitually assume that productivity will pick up. Based on these unjustified hopes the trend growth rates of the UK and the US are assumed to be much higher than those indicated by the trends of the past five years and the growth of the capital stock. The post-crisis recovery is universally derided as being unsatisfactory, so the prospect of it deteriorating further should be a matter of major concern and be given a suitable degree of attention by economists and in the financial press. This is not, however, yet the case. Rather than being a central issue for the economy, it has proved to be difficult to get press and public attention focused on the problem. There has been some public discussion about the views of Robert Gordon compared with those of optimists such as Joel Mokyr,[2] but these revolve around hopes that TFP will improve and fears that it won't. Since we can neither know whether hopes will be dupes or fears liars, nor take measures to affect the result, the debate is

---

[1] Gordon (2016).   [2] Mokyr (2016).

irrelevant from the viewpoint of policy. Unfortunately it distracts attention from the debate which should be occurring, which is how to boost growth independently of changes in TFP. Problems are unlikely to be solved unless they attract general concern and possible solutions are widely debated. We should therefore be worried that there is so little discussion about our weak growth potential and try to understand why this has happened and then rectify it.

One persistent problem is that growth is largely discussed in terms of technology rather than investment. The threat that we will soon be replaced by machines attracts much more attention than the problem that this is not happening fast enough to boost productivity. Technical advances that can be imagined usually happen, but there was a gap of six hundred years between Roger Bacon suggesting that we could fly and the first aeroplanes; and we still do not have an economic way of producing electricity from the power of fusion, despite heavy expenditure of effort and money spread over several decades. The widely perceived threat from technology seems to assume that robots do not have to be built or maintained, only imagined. If today's technology were fully utilized, there would be no emerging economies as they would have already caught up with fully developed ones. Technology is underused in emerging countries, partly because of lower levels of education but also because the necessary investment has not yet been made. Even in the most advanced economy the average level of applied technology is well below the best, and productivity would advance sharply in the UK and the US without any advance in technology if the average level approached the best more closely. It is the slow rate at which today's technology is being put in place that is our current problem, not the threat that it will put us all out of work.

Developments in technology are habitually reported with a negative spin. A recent article remarked that 'researchers at McKinsey . . . estimate that almost half of global activities will be replaced by a robot within the next two decades'.[3] If true this would almost certainly be good news, as it would boost productivity and thus allow a much needed acceleration in real wages. It would only be bad if it led to widespread unemployment, which would only be necessary if there were a rise in the rate of unemployment consistent with stable inflation (NAIRU).[4] Demand can always be stimulated to maintain full employment, and in the absence of a rise in the NAIRU, full employment would be at the same level as it is today. In today's financial reporting two

---

[3] Tett (2017).
[4] The level of unemployment which is compatible with a stable level of inflation is known as the non-accelerating inflation rate of unemployment (NAIRU).

biases are in conflict. It seems assumed that technology is about to destroy employment, yet that unemployment can have a further sustained fall without inflation becoming a threat. If the latter is correct, fiscal and monetary stimuli will be able to sustain full employment without generating inflation.

This distraction is a nuisance, but there are many other barriers to debate which serve to reinforce complacency. I touched in Chapter 1 on a number of these, including the one I labelled as the 'post hoc ergo propter hoc fallacy'. When an idea is generally assumed to be true, it largely ceases to be discussed. Many people are then irritated if asked to rethink the point, as the request carries with it the implied criticism that they have been naive in accepting the conventional view too readily. Reluctance to reconsider ideas is reinforced by those who have been wrong in their past judgements through such inadequate scepticism. Economists and financial journalists who have assumed that the slow growth of the post-crisis economy was the result of the crisis have generally fallen into this trap. Unless the weak recent expansion has causes which date from before the crisis, it is hard to see how they can be due to anything except insufficient demand. The post hoc fallacy thus led, while the recent recovery was under way, to calls for less fiscal stringency in the UK and the US on the grounds that this was keeping resources unused and preventing a full recovery. The rapid fall in unemployment is proof that they were wrong. But the natural dislike of accepting their errors has inhibited those who argued for more fiscal stimulus from discussing why they were wrong. The excessive prominence and praise given to those who make good forecasts stimulates denial by those who make bad ones, and encourages ways of avoiding this key point. If we did not place such exaggerated emphasis on economic forecasting, we should find it easier to accept that little blame attaches to the resulting errors. The attribution of blame should be limited to those who are foolish enough to think that making forecasts is the key purpose of economics and to those who are unwilling to admit error when they get their forecasts wrong.

Because we attach too much importance to one-off forecasts, the press is full of articles by those seeking to exculpate themselves from the blame of having made poor ones. The error made by those who called for more stimuli to demand was not that the UK and US economies grew more rapidly than they expected, but that they failed to notice that these economies' capacity to grow had been seriously curtailed. Unwillingness to admit error has served to hide this key distinction and has led to the widespread denial that trend growth has fallen and to a wish to believe that additional demand will conjure up additional supply to match it. The number and prominence of those in denial about their error has led to a wide, though seemingly unconsidered, acceptance of this complacent attitude. It is still widely believed that productivity has been temporarily depressed and will soon recover.

Table 18. Forecasts of UK labour productivity by the OBR compared with historical outturn (percentage increase per annum) (Data sources: OBR and ONS (ABMI and YBUS)

	For 2016	For 2020
Forecast November 2015	1.5%	2.2%
Forecast November 2016	1.3%	1.8%
Forecast November 2017	0.9%[5]	1.2%[6]
Change in GDP per hour over 5 years to Q4 2017 % p.a.	0.77%	

Table 19. Forecasts of US labour productivity by the CBO compared with historical outturn (percentage increase per annum) (Data sources: CBO, NIPA Table 1.1.6 and BLS Table b10)

	For 2017 to 2027
Forecast June 2015	1.8%
Forecast June 2017	1.5%
Change in GDP per hour over 5 years to Q4 2017	0.57%

The UK's Office of Budget Responsibility (OBR) is a non-partisan body charged with making economic assessments as a check on government budget plans. As Table 18 shows, the OBR has revised down its assumptions for labour productivity, but even the downward revisions made in 2017 still assume that labour productivity will be much higher than that recorded over the past five years.

In the US the Congressional Budget Office (CBO) fulfils a similar rôle and I set out its forecasts in Table 19. Even more than in the UK the expectations for productivity appear unrealistic when compared with the results of the past five years.

On both sides of the Atlantic fiscal policy has thus been and continues to be based on assumptions which remain optimistic even after being revised down. Almost anything is possible in economics, so productivity could suddenly jump, but it is also possible that it will deteriorate further. While we can hope that things will get better, it is clearly imprudent to base our plans and policies on the assumption that productivity will now improve sharply in the absence of new policies designed to achieve it.

The sharp falls in unemployment and labour productivity make it clear that we have a problem with supply rather than demand. Among the various other ways used to avoid the conclusions that naturally follow, one frequently encountered is a refusal to consider the problems of individual economies and instead to claim that on a worldwide basis we have unused resources and

---

[5] For 2017.   [6] For 2022.

that a boost to demand is therefore needed. This manages to be both correct and irrelevant to the problems of the UK and US economies. There can be little doubt that the Eurozone suffers from inadequate demand, with 10.8 per cent unemployment compared with the OECD's average of 6.8 per cent. Fiscal stimulus in the Eurozone would be a boon for everybody, but fiscal stimulus everywhere would not be. It is unhelpful to treat the world as if it were one economy, and sad that attention can be diverted from the specific and differing needs of individual economies by doing so, as in particular it loses sight of the key issue of weak supply. One reason such diversions are often successful is that there is a bias in academic economics in favour of universal models, which leads to a relative lack of attention to work devoted to the gritty and time-consuming labour of studying economic data in detail. The extent of this bias is demonstrated by the fact that Cambridge University, which has many chairs in economics, has had none in applied economics. Cambridge has at last raised the necessary funds to finance one. This is encouraging and I hope that this shows that the bias of academics against applied economics is beginning to change.

The recent combination of weak growth and falling unemployment is a unique event in the post-war era. Before we entered this period, weak growth meant inadequate demand, and when demand was boosted then weak growth came to an end. Public debate over economic policy was therefore almost solely concerned with keeping demand at a level which avoided either unemployment or inflation. When this was achieved, economies grew at an adequate pace and there was no need to worry. An almost automatic assumption that this must always be the case has become inbuilt, and now that it is no longer true it is difficult to overcome. Even though the fall in unemployment shows that demand has been fully adequate, it has been widely assumed that recent weak growth must have been an issue of demand, and a number of theories have been produced to explain a non-existent problem. Some of these ideas are based on claims that are simply untenable; others provided possible explanations of why demand has been constrained in the European Union, but not why this has been accompanied by weak supply in the UK and the US. These various explanations provide no insights to account for the changes in either demographics or productivity, and thus shed no light on the decline in the growth of output potential.

It has been observed that, in the past, financial crises have regularly been followed by periods of weak growth.[7] Financial crises are a great shock in which borrowers default on many debts. This produces a sudden loss of wealth for the lenders, who therefore try to increase their net savings by cutting back

---

[7] Reinhart and Rogoff (2009).

on expenditure. They also become more cautious about the use of their savings and less willing to lend to risky borrowers or provide them with equity finance. At the same time those borrowers become increasingly worried that they will not be able to secure the funds they need to refinance old debts or raise new ones. Thus both borrowers and lenders seek to increase their savings and cut back on their investments. This is the problem identified by John Maynard Keynes, of intentions to save outrunning intentions to invest. As the two must match after the event, the economy must adjust so that savings equal investment. This can be achieved either by falls in incomes and output, which thwart the intentions to save, or by the government running budget deficits, whereby the excess savings of the private sector are absorbed by the 'negative savings' of the public sector.

Financial crises thus cause recessions, for reasons that fit Keynes's analysis. The last one was true to form, being followed by the great recession of 2008. It should therefore be no surprise that financial crises have been followed by periods of weak demand and, when there has been an absence of offsetting fiscal stimuli, by weak growth. This does not, however, explain why the recession should have been followed by a slowdown in the growth of potential output (and this is not usually claimed). It is likely that the shock given by the financial crisis contributed to the drop in investment that occurred in both the UK and the US from 2008 to 2010, and it may have had a lasting impact in constraining the relative weak recovery in investment that has occurred since. Had this fall resulted in a period of high and sustained unemployment it might have damaged productivity by reducing the subsequent ability to work of those who suffered as a result of the crisis. But as Figure 17 illustrates, there was no unusually prolonged period of high unemployment following the financial crisis. Both the UK and the US had five years from 2009 to 2014 in which unemployment was over 6 per cent, but this level was also exceeded in the UK for twenty years from 1980 to 1999 and in the US, except for a brief respite in 1979 when unemployment fell to 5.85 per cent, from 1975 to 1987.

If investment remains at its current depressed level the growth potential of the major Anglophone economies will remain poor, but the impact of the low level of recent investment is trifling compared with the impact of the falls in the level of investment that have taken place over the past thirty to forty years and which, combined with the fall in the ratio of tangible to intangible investment, have led to the slowdown in the growth of the net capital stock, as I illustrated in Figures 4 and 5.

The current level of investment is the subject of much misinformation. It is sometimes claimed that it has 'recovered'. But this is only true in the sense that investment is higher than it was at its trough in the recession. But net investment in the UK has fallen by 35 per cent from its peak and by 65 per cent in the US. Claiming that investment has recovered is the equivalent of asserting that a test batsman has recovered his form if he succeeds in mildly troubling the scorers after a string of ducks, or a top tennis player who manages to win one game in a match after a series of whitewashes. Even if investment were to recover it will, unfortunately, need to be sustained for several years at a much higher level than today. Only then will the stock of relatively up-to-date equipment start to rise again at the speed necessary to improve labour productivity to the extent that living standards rise rapidly enough to meet the reasonable aspirations of voters.

Another distraction, which diverts attention away from serious debate about our problems, is the misleading claim that companies are not investing because they wish to reduce their debt levels. This has been branded by its exponents as a 'balance sheet recession'. This brings forcibly to mind comments about a speaker of whom it was remarked that 'he said some new things and some true things. Unfortunately the true things were not new and the new things were not true'. It is true but not new to claim that the wish to reduce debt levels can constrain investment. This is simply a restatement of part of the standard Keynesian analysis. It is therefore reasonable, if far from new, to claim that a wish to repair balance sheets can depress investment and consumption and thus cause recessions. The new but not true bit is that a balance sheet recession can account for the current low level of investment. Had US companies wished to improve their balance sheets they would not have bought shares and thus increased their leverage. As Figure 48 shows, US

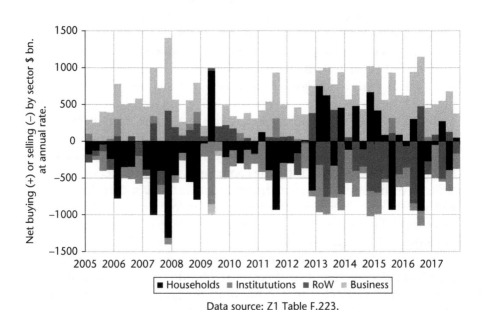

Data source: Z1 Table F.223.

Figure 48. US: Equity buying by sector

non-financial companies bought shares in every quarter since 2005, with the exception of the second and third quarters of 2009. As Figure 43 shows, they have cut back on their capital spending but increased their cash distributions to shareholders through dividends and buy-backs. As Figure 25 shows, they have been increasing, not reducing, their debt ratios, using these additional funds to help finance the higher level of dividends and buy-backs.

The claim that growth has been held back by the wish to reduce debt is contrary to the evidence worldwide as well as in the US. There does not seem to have been any debt reduction nor has debt appeared to be a constraint on the growth of demand. 'The great irony of the Great Financial Crisis is that a crisis borne out of indebtedness has spawned even more leverage in its wake. In fact, debt has never before increased this rapidly in peacetime. However, contrary to popular belief, it has not *yet* created a serious drag on global growth.'[8]

---

[8] Pradhan, Goodhart and Drozdzik (2016).

19

Deflation

Comments about the dangers of deflation are another way in which discussion has been diverted away from the essential problem of slow trend growth. The premise is that deflation causes recessions, which is simply not true. Deflation can be a symptom of inadequate demand but it can also occur when demand is strong. The fallacy comes from ignoring history and the importance of inflationary expectations.

Inflation is expected to fall when unemployment is below the non-accelerating inflationary rate of unemployment (NAIRU), or even at that level if inflationary expectations are weak. In addition to unemployment and expectations there are other influences on the price level, such as international commodity prices and the exchange rate. But these mostly have a short-term impact and are unlikely to have had a noticeable effect over thirty years.

Prices fell in both the UK and the US from 1870 to 1900, as I illustrate in Figures 49 and 50. Over the same period growth was robust in both countries, as Tables 20 and 21 show.

In the UK growth in both GDP and GDP per head accelerated compared with the previous fifty years.[1] The total growth of the US economy was slightly slower from 1870 to 1900 than it had been over the previous fifty years, but this was more than accounted for by the slowdown in the growth of population. As Table 21 shows, the improvement in living standards, defined as GDP per head, accelerated sharply. The period from 1870 to 1900 has been termed a depression, despite the strong rise in living standards, due to the sharp fall in prices notably of agricultural commodities. This was particularly severe on the US farming population, which in 1900 accounted for 41 per cent of all those employed, but much less of a problem in the UK, where by 1901 only

---

[1] The year 1820 is the first in the nineteenth century for which data for UK and US GDP are available: see Maddison (2003).

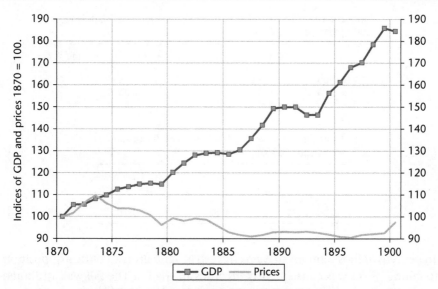

Data sources: Angus Maddison & C.H. Feinstein.

Figure 49. UK: Growth with deflation 1870 to 1900

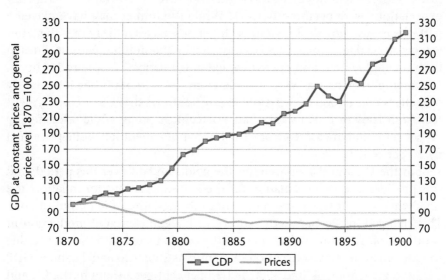

Data sources: Angus Maddison & NBER.

Figure 50. US: Growth with deflation 1870 to 1900

Table 20. UK GDP and GDP per head (Data sources: Maddison (2003); Feinstein (1976))

	GDP % p.a. change	GDP per head % p.a. change
1870 to 1900	2.06	1.15
1820 to 1870	2.05	0.87

Table 21. US GDP and GDP per head (Data source: Maddison (2003))

	GDP	GDP per head
1870 to 1900	3.93	1.73
1820 to 1870	4.20	1.18

15 per cent of those employed were engaged in agriculture.[2] Political opposition to falling prices was consequently vigorous in the US. The fall was attributed to the US adherence to the gold standard and was made famous in the rhetoric of the twice-failing presidential candidate William Jennings Bryan, with his cry 'You shall not crucify mankind upon a cross of gold'.

There are two possible explanations for the long period of falling prices. Either unemployment was regularly above the NAIRU or inflationary expectations were persistently weak. While the former may have played a part, the robust growth shown in both periods makes it likely that the latter was a powerful influence. This is supported by the simultaneous declines in both unemployment and prices over extended periods. As Figure 51 shows, UK unemployment was very volatile from 1870 to 1900 but fell slightly over the whole period of deflation. Figure 52 shows that US unemployment rose from 1869 to 1900 by less than a percentage point, while prices fell by 26 per cent, and, measured from 1874, unemployment fell while prices fell by 15 per cent.[3]

Both the UK and the US were on the gold standard over this period, and this provides a ready explanation for the low expectations for inflation at a time when output was rising much more strongly than the output of gold. This changed in the twentieth century with significant gold production in South Africa. The faster fall in prices in the US compared with the UK was due to differences in the growth of productivity. As Tables 20 and 21 show, GDP per head grew from 1870 to 1900 at 1.15 per cent per annum in the UK and

[2] Data from Bureau of the Census, *Historical Statistics of the United States*, and Feinstein (1976). No doubt the proportions employed in agriculture were even higher in the preceding thirty years, for which I have been unable to find data.
[3] My data for US unemployment are from Vernon (1994), which I have extended to 1900 using BLS data for the change in the level from 1899.

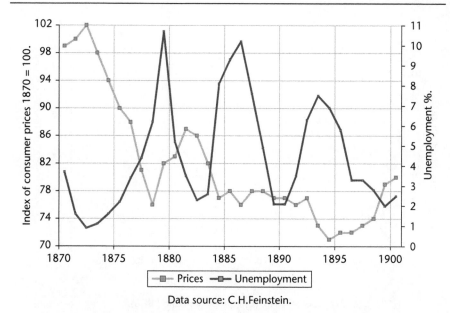

Data source: C.H.Feinstein.

Figure 51. UK: Prices and unemployment 1870 to 1900

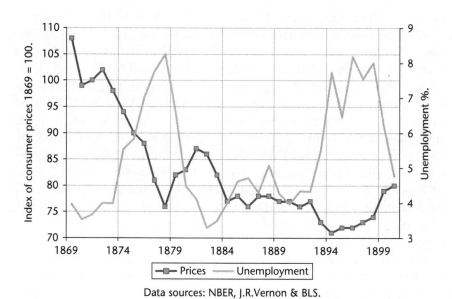

Data sources: NBER, J.R.Vernon & BLS.

Figure 52. US: Prices and unemployment 1869 to 1900

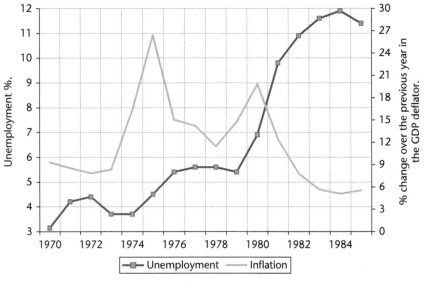

Data source: ONS. (Unemployment and YBGB).

Figure 53. UK Unemployment and inflation 1970 to 1985

1.73 per cent per annum in the US. A country whose productivity grows more rapidly than another's will have a relative rise in its real exchange rate. As both the UK and the US had exchange rates fixed to gold, it was only through a relatively faster rate of deflation for the US that this could have occurred.[4]

After depressing inflation in the last thirty years of the nineteenth century, expectations had the opposite impact after the oil shock. From 1970 to 1985 UK inflation was highly volatile but fell over the period as a whole, while unemployment, as Figure 53 shows, rose from 3.2 per cent to 11.4 per cent. There were periods such as 1970 to 1973 in which inflation fell and unemployment rose, and also periods when they both rose together such as 1974 to 1976 and 1978 to 1980. But the fundamental problem was the exceptionally large rise in unemployment that was needed to bring inflation under control.

Figure 54 shows that the situation was very similar in the US over the same period.

In both the UK and the US, inflation has recently been more subdued than forecasters have anticipated. The most likely reason is that expectations have remained low, as they did in the late nineteenth century. Output then grew under conditions of full employment while prices declined; today, low expectations for inflation have allowed stable prices to be combined with falling unemployment.

---

[4] This is known in economic theory as the Balassa–Samuelson effect. For a fuller explanation see Appendix 6.

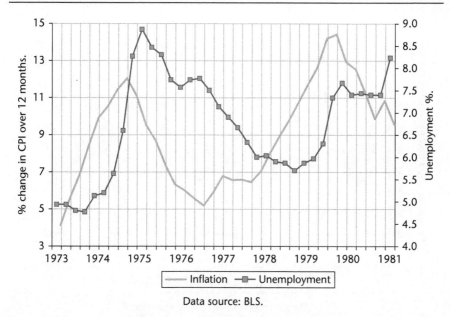

Data source: BLS.

Figure 54. US: Inflation and unemployment

If unemployment continues to fall, then at some point both inflation and its expectations will start to rise. This level is unknown, and there is another uncertainty: whether the short-term NAIRU level, at which inflation starts to pick up, will be same as the minimum level of unemployment needed subsequently to keep inflation from accelerating. (Short-term and medium-term NAIRU are unlikely to be the same.)

If expectations change suddenly when inflation starts to increase, the level of unemployment compatible with stable inflation is likely to rise sharply. Unfortunately a sudden change is probable, as it seems that inflationary expectations are very volatile. The Bank of England publishes estimates based on changes in the yields on nominal government bonds, and those are linked to inflation. They show that the expected change in inflation over the next two years moved from minus 3 per cent to plus 3 per cent between 1990 and 1991.[5] Changes in expectations are also volatile from month to month, and rises and falls are regularly reversed quickly. We cannot therefore be sure that a marked change has occurred before it is too late for inflation to be controlled by a gentle change in monetary policy. Once started, a rise in expectations will probably need to be contained by dramatic increases in interest rates. This was the medicine applied by Paul Volcker when Chairman of the Federal Reserve, as I show in Figure 55. Under his guidance policy rates

[5] See Breedon (1995), Figures 4, 5, and 6.

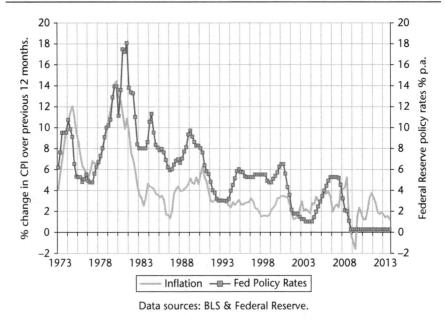

Data sources: BLS & Federal Reserve.

Figure 55. US: Inflation and Federal Reserve policy rates

rose to 18 per cent in 1981 and remained well above inflation as it fell until 2002. The policy was successful at the cost of a sharp recession, with unemployment rising to nearly 11 per cent in 1982.

The US economy was in far better shape in 1982 to withstand a shock increase in interest rates than it is today. Table 22 shows that both leverage and share prices are much higher today than they were in 1982, with the consequence that the economy is much more vulnerable to a sharp rise in interest rates. The danger now is that even much milder increases in interest rates than those which occurred under Paul Volcker could set off a large fall in the stock market and in the prices of other financial assets. This would cause a sharp fall in demand and profits, setting off fears—followed by the reality—of widespread debt defaults. High asset prices and debt levels render the economy today particularly susceptible to a shock rise in interest rates.

An added risk today is that the volatility of inflationary expectations is likely to have increased because of quantitative easing (QE), which involves the purchase of long-dated government bonds by central banks financed by short-term borrowing. But central banks are part of the public sector, thus QE amounts to a reduction in the proportion of government debt which is financed on a long-term rather than a short-term basis. Over the past one hundred years or more the cost of long-term debt has been significantly greater than that of short-term debt. Long-term funding is expensive; the key question is therefore 'Why do governments fund long-term?' Either they

Table 22. Comparing 1982 and 2017 in the US (Data sources: Z1 Table D3, NIPA Table 1.1.5, Z1 Table B.102, and Stephen Wright)

	Q4 1982	Q4 2017
Household debt as percentage of GDP	47%	77%
Non-financial business debt as percentage of GDP	53%	72%
Financial debt as percentage of GDP	24%	81%
Stock market value[6] according to q	41% undervalued	84% overvalued

are costing taxpayers money without reward or there is in fact a benefit. The most obvious one is that long-term funding makes fiscal deficits less volatile. If, for example, debt equals GDP and is funded long-term, there is no change in government spending if interest rates rise; but if it is funded short-term then a rise of 1 per cent in interest rates will produce a rise of 1 per cent in government expenditure and (even with some resulting increase in tax revenue) it is likely to produce a large rise in the fiscal deficit. As increases in the fiscal deficit stimulate demand, and central banks' purpose in raising interest rates is to dampen demand, countries in which governments fund short will need sharper than usual increases in interest rates to constrain demand. QE thus amplifies the risk of central banks being insufficiently hawkish, and it is therefore rational for inflationary expectations to become more volatile, given the massive amount of central bank buying of long-term debt which we have seen in recent years. A rise in public sector interest payments could be avoided by requiring banks to hold deposits with the central bank at low or zero interest rates, but only at the risk of bankrupting them.

Central banks aim to achieve a stable inflation rate of 2 per cent without recessions. This may not be possible if the short and medium-term levels of NAIRU are different; even if not impossible it is likely to be difficult. As we have had periodic recessions without long gaps between them, history provides no sustained example of central banks' success: policy should therefore allow for the asymmetry between the risks of different errors. While acting too early or too strongly will cause unemployment to rise, this can be easily reversed by a change in policy. The consequences of delayed or weak action are more serious. Once expectations have taken off, the level of unemployment compatible with stable inflation will rise and policy would have to tighten—and could not then readily be reversed, as a serious recession would be needed to bring inflation and its expectations back under control.

---

[6] The US equity market can be valued either as proposed by Robert Shiller (2000) using the cyclically adjusted price–earnings ratio or as proposed by Stephen Wright and me (Smithers and Wright 2000) using the q ratio of market to replacement value. Figure 27 shows that they produce similar results. I have used q here as it gives the lower of the two current measures of overvaluation and thus the lower estimate of the current level of risk.

Central banks should therefore err on the side of tightening too soon rather than too late, but this will be difficult and unpopular, partly because the excessive optimism about the trend level of growth in the UK and the US discourages timely increases in interest rates. Those who have often (and wrongly) blamed deflation for causing depressions see low inflation as a sign of incipient doom, and this has led some economists to call for central banks to raise their target rate for inflation. History shows that deflation does not cause recessions, though it can be a symptom of them, but this distinction appears too subtle to be widely accepted. Public opinion, as voiced by politicians and the popular and even the financial press, is therefore likely to press for economic stimuli until prices rise to target levels, at which point unemployment may already be below the level needed to keep inflationary expectations in check once they have started to rise.

It is often asserted that falling prices cause consumers to postpone their spending in the expectation of further falls, and that the fall in demand will thereby lead to recession. This is not supported by experience. Even if the assumptions about expectations were always correct, which is unlikely, this approach ignores the many other ways in which deflation can affect consumer incomes and behaviour. In practice rising prices are more likely to depress spending than falling ones. It is observed that wages are 'stickier' than prices, in that they move less readily. Employee incomes therefore tend to rise in the short-term as a proportion of output when prices fall. Consumer demand would thus also rise if the savings' rate did not rise, which history shows to be unlikely. As I illustrate in Figure 56, personal savings in the US have risen with inflation and fallen back when it declines; this pattern is found both during the deflation of the 1930s and the inflation of the post-war era.[7]

People can hold their cash in banknotes, and although this is inconvenient and, if the notes are to be held safely, involves some cost, it means that it is difficult for interest rates to fall much below zero.[8] This provides another argument against deflation, because it prevents real interest rates from becoming significantly negative and it is often assumed that negative real interest rates will boost investment. This assumption is testable but proves to be wrong when tested. It seems that investment responds to nominal rather than real interest rates, so no further encouragement can be given today when interest rates are near zero.[9] If domestic demand is inadequate when interest rates are around zero, it needs to be boosted by fiscal rather than monetary policy.

The Eurozone—where demand is inadequate and responds weakly to lower interest rates—would benefit from a fiscal policy boost. But this has

---

[7] The R^2 correlation is 0.32.

[8] It is difficult but not impossible, as banknotes could, for example, have a date on them and then become valueless unless a payment for their renewal is made.

[9] See Appendix 1.

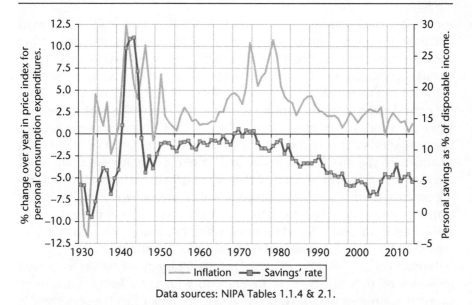

Data sources: NIPA Tables 1.1.4 & 2.1.

Figure 56. US: Personal savings and inflation

not been the situation recently in the UK and the US, where full employment has been accompanied by low inflation. It is possible that even lower unemployment might encourage investment, if employing more people became increasingly difficult and expensive. This is put forward as a case for delaying plans for fiscal or monetary tightening even if unemployment were to continue to fall. There are two objections to this. The first is that it is very doubtful whether investment would be appreciably boosted. The second is that it would be very risky. When assessing possible policies to boost investment, we should consider their costs and the damage which they might do in other ways. This key consideration has often been ignored. If a policy poses few if any risks to the economy, it should rank high in our priorities. The best policies will have high prospects of success and present few risks of damaging the economy. The next preference should be for policies whose success is less certain but which have low risks. High-risk policies should be avoided, just as doctors should seek to do no harm with their medication.

In February 2018 inflation, as measured by the change in the CPI over the past twelve months, was 2.7 per cent in the UK and 2.2 per cent in the US and thus above a 2 per cent target. Problems are unlikely to arise if inflation remains for a while above target. It is, however, vital to prevent a rise in inflationary expectations.

The anxiety about deflation has been an influence on monetary policy. My main concern is that excessive ease in the past has driven up asset prices and encouraged the build-up of debt, and that this will now lead via a rise in inflationary expectations to making the next recession a severe one. Other concerns have been voiced by many highly respected economists. These include Claudio Borio,[10] who heads the Monetary and Economic Department of the Bank of International Settlements (BIS); Charles Goodhart, former Bank of England Chief Economist and an erstwhile member of the Bank of England Monetary Policy Committee; Mervyn King, former Governor of the Bank of England; and William White, previously the chief economist of the BIS and chairman of the OECD's Economic and Development Review Committee. Among the risks against which they warn are that financial institutions, including banks and life insurance companies, will be increasingly liable to default as their profitability will be eroded by an extended period of low interest rates. It is also likely that getting back to normal will be increasingly difficult and risky the longer the period of abnormal monetary policy continues.[11]

Another concern over the results of excessive easy money is due to varying responses by different types of investment, with some being much more strongly stimulated than investment generally. When this happens there is a risk that asset prices—whose rise encouraged the excesses—will collapse, not only bringing down investment in that particular area but causing more general problems through widespread debt default. This is termed malinvestment, and Mervyn King, in particular, has emphasized the risks that it poses.[12]

Prior to the financial crisis, malinvestment occurred in many countries. There was over-investment in housing in Ireland, Spain and the US. More recently there has been excessive investment in raw material production. Malinvestment is hard to identify before a crisis, but one current concern is that it may be found in commercial property, as low interest rates do not stimulate all types of investment equally but have a notably strong impact on property. This imbalance is exacerbated today as the perverse incentives of the bonus culture discourage investment in business equipment. Ultra-easy credit not only encourages the high levels of debt and asset prices, which are the usual cause of financial crises, it also pushes up the prices of the existing stock of property and the speed at which new space is being built. This is a dangerous combination, as a rapid rate of building increases the probability that supply will become excessive and will take years to work off, while the boost to prices makes it likely that when they fall they will fall a long way. This combination in residential property set off the financial crisis and today commercial property seems to provide an obvious risk.

The concerns that current monetary policy is leading to malinvestment, and weakness in both banks and insurance companies, all relate to the important task of preventing another financial crisis.

---

[10] Borio, Gambacorta and Hofmann (2015).   [11] White (2015).   [12] King (2016).

20

The UK Is Similar to the US

Since 1995 the UK economy has followed a very similar path to that of the US. Investment had fallen sharply from peak levels in both countries and this decline started well before 2008. These declines in investment caused the subsequent slow growth in net capital stock and labour productivity.

As in the US, there was a dramatic rise in management pay. Incentive payments, as shown in Figure 57, rose five times between 1997 and 2008. It thus seems extremely probable that the decline in investment and productivity in the UK was also the result of the perverse incentives of the bonus culture. Unfortunately we do not have data to test the relationship between investment corporation tax and RoE in the UK as is shown for the US in Figures 39 and 40. We do however have evidence that, as in the US, large

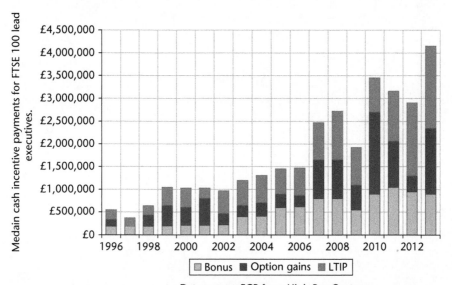

Data source: ECR from High Pay Centre
"No routine riches" May 2015 (by inspection).

Figure 57. UK: Management cash incentive payments 1996 to 2013

companies in the UK have been the main cause of the decline in investment and productivity.[1]

It is possible that the changes in UK corporate tax may have also contributed to the sharp fall in investment. The situation in the UK is much more complicated than in the US as there have been changes not only in the rate of corporation tax but in the system used. In 1997 the Chancellor of the Exchequer, Gordon Brown, abolished the existing system of advanced corporation tax and a traditional corporation tax system was imposed in its place. This had the effect of increasing the effective rate of corporation tax very sharply,[2] though press comment at the time shows that this was not generally understood. Had the increase been maintained its effect would probably have become more apparent and would have depressed investment; in practice, however, there seems to have been little short-term impact and subsequent changes have brought the effective rate back to its pre-1997 level.

The vote to leave the European Union is likely to depress real living standards and thus amplify the problem.

---

[1] For the US see Asker, Farre-Mensa and Ljungqvist (2015) and for the UK see Riley, Rincon-Aznar and Samek (2018).

[2] I set out the details in Appendix 7.

21

Reversing Perverse Incentives

The depressed level of business investment prevents the UK and US economies from achieving a satisfactory level of growth. There are two possible ways to change this. The first is to change the way senior managers are remunerated. The second is to leave the incentives unchanged but alter their impact on investment.

The first route requires that incentives are changed from those that hurt the economy to those that help it, and we could try to enforce this or at least seek to encourage it. The choice is between proscription and persuasion, either by passing laws which would make it illegal to have 'unsatisfactory' remuneration structures, or by encouraging companies to have satisfactory ones through the incentives of publicity and tax. As a general rule, persuasion is likely to be both more acceptable and more effective than proscription. It has the additional advantage of being more easily adapted to the particular circumstances of individual companies, and is less likely therefore to meet reasoned opposition based on the probability that any change will have unanticipated impacts. The tax system could be readily adapted to produce a change to bonus systems so that they encourage companies to improve productivity rather than discourage them from doing so. We could delegate to competition authorities the power to approve bonus systems for companies over a certain size. They are the appropriate bodies to judge these schemes because, as I have shown, the damage done to economies through perverse incentives is similar to the damage done by inadequate levels of competition.

The following principles might apply.

(i) Approvals should be conditional on bonuses only being paid if the company improved its productivity by a given amount, such as 1 per cent each year.

(ii) Companies need not have their remuneration schemes accepted, but should be encouraged to seek approval through tax incentives. Without the authorities' stamp of approval incentive payments should not be a deductible expense for corporation tax.

(iii)   To simplify things, this should apply only to those earning more than, say, $250,000 or its sterling equivalent a year. This would also avoid interfering with schemes designed for lower-level employees.

(iv)   For example, if the marginal rate of corporation tax were 35 per cent, the fall in profits after tax that results from an incentive payment of $1,000,000 would be the full cost of the payment rather than $650,000, which would be the cost if the bonuses were tax deductible.

(v)   It would probably be even more effective if there were a levy, equal to say 80 per cent, applicable to unapproved incentive payments, so that the company would have to pay $800,000 to the tax authorities in addition to the $1,000,000 it paid to individuals and none of the $1,800,000 would be an allowable expense for corporation tax.

(vi)   A high level of tax on unapproved bonuses should be particularly effective. A bonus of $1,000,000 might normally be subject to (say) 35 per cent tax and the recipient would then receive $650,000 net of tax, but unapproved benefits might be taxed at 80 per cent leaving the recipient with only $200,000 after tax.

(vii)   Achieving the productivity target should not be the only metric for calculating incentive payments, but should be an addition to the profit-type targets currently used. Shareholders want some benefit, or at least the appearance of it, in return for the bonuses their companies pay to management; approved incentive schemes should therefore involve adding to profit criteria rather than replacing them.

(viii)   This approach should, among its other benefits, ease the political difficulty of reform. Together these two criteria should severely limit the ability of companies to meet targets by disposing of parts of their business with low productivity, as this would almost invariably be costly and thus increase the difficulty of meeting the profit levels needed for incentive payments.

The cost of introducing a productivity target into company schemes should be minimal, because companies already have the information they need. However, it is seldom if ever published—a failure that is both the result and the cause of misinformation: a requirement to publish the necessary data would on its own benefit the economy. Productivity is the output that a country or a company produces per hour worked. The rate at which productivity improves is the single most important factor in determining the future prosperity of a country. It is also a matter of vital importance to individual companies. Companies have to pay wages which are competitive with those offered by other companies and which are therefore determined nationally. For the economy as a whole, wages increase over time rise in line with the rate at which productivity improves: the wages paid by individual companies are thus determined by the rate at which they rise nationally. Individual companies cannot avoid paying higher wages if wages are rising generally. Companies whose productivity lags thus face a major problem. They will either have to raise their prices faster than the general price rise, and consequently be at risk of being undercut by competitors, or they will find their profits falling.

Despite its importance, most managements and shareholders are completely in the dark about the levels and changes in productivity of the companies they run or own. Shareholders and investment banks can only analyse published data. The questions they pose are thus restricted to these data, and there is a natural tendency for managements to assume that these are the important ones. The failure to publish output and productivity data has the effect of making them seem trivial. The requirement to publish should therefore have a beneficial effect on the attitude of managements and shareholders by alerting them to the importance of improving productivity. What is measured gets managed and what is not measured is ignored.

Productivity is the ratio between the hours worked by employees and the company's output. Companies have to know how much they pay their staff, including the cost of their salaries, pensions and other benefits, and the hours they work, or are assumed to do so under their contracts. Output can be easily measured because it is the cost of employing people plus profits, measured before depreciation, interest and tax. Companies must therefore know their output, even though they don't publish it. They must also know how many staff they employ and, in order to pay them in accordance with their contracts, the number of hours they work. As these two necessary pieces of information are already known, the cost of publishing them in annual reports must be nearly zero. If published they will show the companies' productivity and, with due allowance for changes in prices, we will then know how each company's productivity changes year by year.

At present companies publish data on their sales but not on their output—though the majority of analysts seem to think that sales measure output. The difference between the two is that output is less than sales by the amount that companies spend on buying services and materials from outside sources. In terms of the national accounts it is the difference between final and intermediate output. If the sales of companies were assumed to measure their output, there would be double counting—for example, when a motor company buys steel and then sells automobiles. The total sales in the economy include the sum of the sales of both steel and cars, but the purchase of the steel by the motor company represents an intermediate rather than a final output and needs to be deducted when calculating GDP. The ratio of sales to output for individual companies, or for the economy as a whole, changes. In the

117

post-war world companies have increasingly been outsourcing activities that they previously carried out for themselves. Factories which formerly had their own canteens and transport, and in which many personnel matters (including pension payments) were carried out internally, have been increasingly employing specialist companies to provide these services. This has had the effect of increasing the ratio of sales in the economy to total output. The process is far from smooth, as it can be interrupted by changes in the opposite direction. For example a company which previously sold its products through independent distributors might decide to own its retail outlets. Another way for intermediate output to fall relative to the total would be through a rise in the percentage of total output from new industries, which buy in a lower than average proportion of their output. Changes in profit margins measured relative to sales can therefore convey misleading information about changes in profitability, even in the short-term, and will almost certainly do so when taken over several years.

In Figure 58 I compare the profit margins of US non-financial companies defined in two different ways. One measures the ratio of profits, before depreciation, interest and tax to sales; the other, using the same definition of profits, measures the ratio of profits to output. The data for the sales/profit

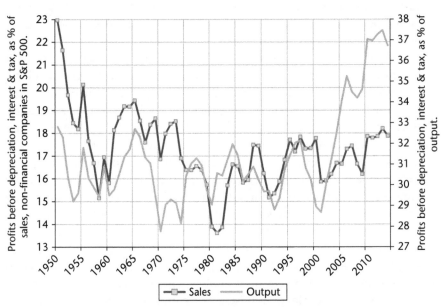

Data sources: Standard & Poor's and NIPA Table 1.14.

Figure 58. US: Non-financial companies comparing profit margins using output and sales

ratio are those of the non-financial members of the S&P 500 going back as far as these data are available, usually from when they first became quoted.[1]

The two series for profit margins are very different, and by comparing the difference between them it is possible to derive an estimate of the ratio between sales and output. Figure 59 shows the result. It indicates that there has been a long trend of growth in the proportion of corporate output bought in from outside sources rather than produced by the companies' own staff and equipment, so that intermediate output and sales have both been rising faster than final output.

Figure 59 also shows that the trend for increased outsourcing has been far from stable, though this may well be exaggerated because the data are for quoted companies. As I have mentioned, one reason why the longer-term trend for increased outsourcing may be interrupted is that new industries can have a level of outsourcing which differs from the average. It seems, for example, that companies like Apple and Google are atypical in this respect. As the composition of the S&P 500 Index changes quite quickly over time and innovative new companies are likely to have high margins in their early years, the impact of these short-term changes in the apparent level of outsourcing is

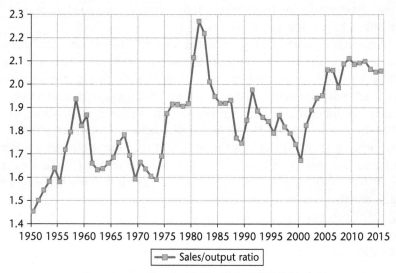

Data sources: Standard & Poor's and NIPA Table 1.14.

Figure 59. US: Non-financial companies' estimated ratio of sales to output

[1] I am grateful to S&P Global Market Intelligence, a division of S&P Global, for providing me with these data and for the help in obtaining and understanding these figures given to me by John Chambers and Georgia Campbell of Standard & Poor's.

Table 23. Illustration of profit and loss accounts showing output as well as sales

Sales (A)	100
Purchases from suppliers (B)	70
Output (C) = (A) minus (B)	30
Employee remuneration (D)	20
Profits, before depreciation, interest & tax (E) = (C) minus (D)	10
Profit margins on sales (E) as percentage of sales (A)	10%
Profit margins on output (D) as percentage of sales (A)	33%

likely to be overstated by the use of quoted company data.[2] While this may affect the short-term fluctuations shown in Figure 59, it seems to me unlikely that it will have significantly distorted any longer-term trends.[3]

Figure 59 shows that that there has been, in accordance with anecdotal evidence, a long-term upward trend in the proportion of corporate output which is outsourced. There is no theoretical reason to assume that profit margins measured with reference to sales will be stable, and the evidence indicates that there has been no such stability. It cannot therefore be sensibly argued that sales margins at any one time are high or low, as such a statement implies some stable longer-term average. Furthermore, even allowing for the proviso I have made, the volatility of profit margins is too great for short-term fluctuations to provide useful information.

An important point, arising from the growth in outsourcing shown in Figure 59, is that published data on the contribution of manufacturing to GDP have tended to overstate the fall. When manufacturing companies out-source such activities as their payroll management and goods distribution, the apparent output of manufacturing falls and that of business services rises.

The long downward trend in profit margins defined in terms of sales, shown in Figure 59, is in marked contrast to the stability of profit margins measured against output shown in Figure 42, which accords with theoretical expect-ations.[4] The publicity given by investment bankers and in the financial press to sales margins is therefore another source of misinformation.

The publication of output data, on the lines illustrated in Table 23, would enable profit margins—which at present can be calculated only as a percent-age of sales—to be calculated also in relation to output.

---

[2] Since 2003, 11 per cent of those currently included by Standard & Poor's as being part of the non-financial constituents of the S&P 500 Index have replaced previous constituents.

[3] The Standard & Poor's data are derived solely from quoted companies and may not therefore provide an accurate guide to changes in the ratio of intermediate to total output for companies in aggregate. Quoted companies appear, however, to produce about 50 per cent of the total output of US companies, so it seems unlikely that the figure gives a misleading impression of the direction of change.

[4] See Appendix 8.

22

Changing the Economic Impact of Current Incentives

To increase investment we must either change incentives on the lines suggested in the previous chapter or leave them unchanged and alter their impact. In a recent discussion Martin Wolf suggested that the simplest way to improve capital spending would be to allow all fixed investment to be accepted as an expense for corporation tax in the year it was made. I had originally thought that this would probably be ineffective so long as current incentives were unchanged. On reflection, however, I have changed my mind as it seems to me that this step would change the response of management to their existing incentives. At present improving EPS or Total Shareholder Return (TSR) are the targets which managements have to achieve to earn bonuses and, as I have explained, under the current tax regime they are met by spending any available cash on dividends and buy-backs rather than fixed tangible investment. A 100 per cent first year's depreciation allowance would change this. The more a company invests the lower will be its tax charge, while the charge for depreciation in its accounts will initially be unchanged. EPS would then rise the more the company invests. As EPS is sometimes the target for bonuses, and usually the driving force behind TSRs, the change in taxation should change the response of management to investment from the negative attitude ruling today to a positive one.

A problem is that the basic rate of corporation tax would need to rise sharply for tax revenue to be unchanged. This has several disadvantages. One is that it would encourage international companies to switch profits to jurisdictions with lower basic rates. Another is that the incentive to buy back shares increases if the basic rate of corporation tax rises. It would therefore be sensible to have a lower rate and maintain revenue by no longer allowing interest to be a deductible expense for corporation tax.

High leverage has been a major cause of financial crises. It is therefore foolish to treat interest as an expense to be deducted when profits are calculated for tax. Both debt and equity provide the capital used to finance investment, and so it would be more sensible to treat them in the same way for tax purposes. The current system encourages companies to use debt rather than equity to finance their operations; they thereby increase their leverage and the risks of financial crises. It would be wise to halt this folly. In addition to this strong case for reform, according to the standard economic model it is likely to have a beneficial impact on investment. Economists typically argue that 'the standard corporate tax base [which allows interest to be deductible] favours debt rather than equity finance, and tends to discourage corporate investment to the extent that companies rely on equity finance'.[1] Money cannot be used for more than one purpose and its use for buy-backs thus competes with its use for investment. Ending the folly of allowing interest to be a deductible expense for corporation tax should, by reducing the benefit of buy-backs to management, make managers more willing to spend money on new investment.

A decline in the cost of debt to small growing businesses should be another benefit of change. At present interest payments are not tax deductible if they vary with the success of the borrowing company. This provision is necessary as otherwise equity could be effectively disguised as debt. After reform, variable interest would have the same tax treatment as a fixed payment. Small companies are often reluctant to issue equity because of the risk that the founding family or partners will lose control of their own creation. Variable interest loans have similarities with equity, but they do not carry voting rights and, unlike non-voting shares, lenders have protection against the misuse of voting power through the fixed value and repayment provisions of debt. If loans with variable interest payments linked to the success of the business became general, the returns on such loans would rise in aggregate unless there were a decline in the average initial rate interest. This would not reduce the total level of interest income, as the payments linked to success would be added to the basic rate. If the market were reasonably competitive, the initial rate would then fall below its previous level. Emerging businesses would then find the initial cost of debt was lower than it otherwise would have been. Their survival rate should rise as they would be less often driven into bankruptcy by the cost of their debt.

Despite the almost universal agreement among economists that interest should cease to be deductible for tax, governments have fought shy of doing so in practice. A proposal for a 'comprehensive business income tax' which would have had this effect was put forward by the US Department of the Treasury in 1992, but the idea seems not to have progressed any further. In

---

[1] Mirrlees et al. (2011).

the UK a change in the system was included in the Conservative Party's programme of 2010, but has since been dropped.

Making interest no longer a deductible expense has four advantages. It reduces the risk of financial crises, it should give some mild boost to investment, it reduces the advantages that accrue to international companies when they shift their profits to tax havens, and it eases the provision of finance to new businesses. Its only drawback is that governments seem unwilling to implement the change. If the tax system were to be reformed on the lines suggested above, the incentives of management would change from deterring investment to actively encouraging it. If this were done, the behaviour of companies should revert to that shown prior to 2000. Tangible investment should then rise in response to the low level of corporation tax and the high level of RoEs.

23

Misinformation Adds to the Risks for the Economy

Steps to arrest the spread of misinformation are valuable. A useful step, even though quite small, would be to insist that companies publish their output data, separating domestic and international figures. The sum of the output data published by companies should equal that shown in the national accounts for the corporate sector. Even if the data were only provided by large companies, the proportion of the total that they represent can be reasonably estimated from other data. If, as seems likely, the output figures from companies proved to be significantly different from those published in the national accounts, the gap would provide us with valuable information— not only about the extent to which companies were currently over or understating their profits, but also on how much this differed from the average overstatement. As national accounts are more reliable than those produced by companies, the extent to which companies were currently misstating profits compared with the long-term average degree of overstatement would provide us with important information. The evidence for an increase in the degree of misstatement is shown by the rise in the volatility of published profits shown in Figure 46. It is likely that profits are now overstated in good times and understated in bad ones. I showed in Table 17 that the current high levels of RoEs published by US quoted companies can only be partly explained by the impact of inflation. It thus seems likely that a significant contribution to the high level of published RoEs comes from profit overstatement. We cannot, however, know the size of this gap because the profits of quoted companies do not necessarily move in step with those for the economy as a whole. The essential information is not the extent to which companies are currently overstating their profits but the extent to which this overstatement is greater than usual. We know by comparing data available from different sources that US quoted companies habitually overstate their published profits.[1]

It is not particularly worrying if companies overstate their profits to the usual extent, because their ratios with historic data will not be affected (as both the current and the average profits will be overstated to the same extent, and it is relative to historic averages that credit risks and market overvaluations are based). But an unusual degree of misstatement is a matter of considerable concern. Overstated RoEs encourages high hurdle rates, thus reducing investment and potential growth, while overstated profits leads to credit risks being understated and encourage debt growth. Overstated profits lower current published PEs and thus encourage overpriced stock markets, contributing to the conditions of high debt and high asset prices which are the key signs of a financially vulnerable economy.

The complacency among respected economists and policymakers about debt and asset prices was a marked feature of public discussion in the run-up to the financial crisis, and was a major contributor to the crisis. Stephen Wright and I attacked this when we warned about the threat of a crisis, and we quoted Alan Blinder who claimed that policymakers would have to lose their heads for another severe recession to occur.[2] We were unkind and unfortunately accurate when we suggested that this was an example of 'the blinder leading the blind'. Similar hubris was shown by Federal Reserve Chairman Ben Bernanke when he claimed that the management of the US economy by the Federal Reserve had improved both its stability and growth.[3] There has happily been a major change of view by many. For example Mervyn King, former Governor of the Bank of England, has blamed the financial crisis on the poor understanding of economics of those who held such complaisant views.[4] I think that he is right and that harm was caused by prominent economists who pooh-poohed those warning of looming problems. Policymakers now seem generally to concur with Mervyn King, and most central banks now agree that they should aim to prevent another financial crisis. Unfortunately the excessively easy monetary policy of quantitative easing has driven up asset prices and, as I explained earlier, has increased the risk of another financial crisis. While avoiding one is not the sole aim of economic policy, it is a necessary condition for policy success.

The concern with financial stability has become known as macroprudential policy. Misinformation has increased the likelihood that attempts to preserve stability through such policy will fail. Falls in asset prices are the usual trigger for financial crises, and the degree to which credit and shares are mispriced should be a key concern for policymakers. If such mispricing is disguised by

---

[1] See Appendix 9. [2] Smithers and Wright (2002). [3] Bernanke (2004).
[4] King (2016).

overstated profits, the tendency will be to underestimate the threat posed by overpriced assets. The exaggerated swing in published profits that will come from the subsequent understatement of profits will accentuate the depth of the subsequent recession.

J. K. Galbraith pointed out that fluctuations in embezzlement had repercussions on the economy.[5] During booms, money is embezzled and in an atmosphere of general euphoria often goes undetected. The result is an increase in the assumed amount of total wealth, as the thieves have the money but their victims have not yet realized the extent of their losses. Once the hard times arrive, the thieves go to jail and the defrauded learn that they are poorer than they thought, so both victims and perpetrators reduce their consumption. Overstating profits has a similar effect but the amounts of money involved are many times those arising from more direct forms of embezzlement. The swings in published profits have a huge impact on the assumed wealth of shareholders. In periods of downturn they exaggerate the profit falls, aggravate the concerns of lenders that they will have not have their loans repaid, and worry borrowers that they will be unable to refinance their debts. These worries by lenders and debtors cause investment to fall and intended savings to rise. Aggravating these changes deepens recessions. The extent of the fall in demand set off by the financial crisis, and the exceptional depth of the subsequent recession, were partly due to the extreme swings in published profits encouraged by the bonus culture.

Modern corporate accounting has contributed to this profit volatility. There has been a change in the valuation of assets from cost to estimated value. By this move from 'marked to cost' to 'marked to value' the element of judgement in accounts has risen relative to more objective assessments. Managements thus have more scope than before to present figures that boost their remuneration. The increased volatility of published profits compared to those in the national accounts provides ample evidence of the extent to which managements used this increased flexibility. Even before the change, however, business and national accounting differed in important respects. Exchanging assets between companies cannot cause profits to rise in aggregate. Such transactions do not and should not have any impact on the profits shown in national accounts. When one company sells an asset to another any profit claimed must be offset by the loss incurred by the other company. If this were reflected in company accounts, corporate and national accounts would agree. This does not happen. Companies which acquire assets are not required to show a loss matching a profit shown by the seller. As inter-company asset transactions have become more frequent this has had an increasing impact.

---

[5] Galbraith (1955).

24

The Economic Consequences
of Higher Investment

There is an urgent need for a rise in the proportion of GDP devoted to tangible investment in the UK and the US. But if we succeed in achieving such an increase, the long-term benefits are likely to have short-term costs, and it will be a painful example of the unavailability of free lunches. Savings are essential to finance capital spending, and as all output is either invested or consumed, a rise in investment as a proportion of GDP requires a compensating fall in the proportion consumed. This is true whether the increases in investment and falls in consumption take place in the private or the public sector. For higher investment to be possible, other changes in the economy must take place. These will probably have to include a rise in taxation, but an increase in private sector savings would reduce the extent of the rise needed and there are reasonable hopes that this would happen.

The need for savings to rise to match investment is certain, but it often seems to be overlooked. A common source of confusion is the assumption that governments can afford more investment because interest rates are so low. This misses the point that in conditions of full employment any increase in investment will stimulate demand, which unless matched by a rise in savings will result in inflation. Only when there is unemployment can governments increase the fiscal deficit without this impact. This applies whether the deficit is boosted by increases in lower taxes or by increased government spending (of any sort, including investment). As it seems likely that unemployment cannot fall much further in either the UK or the US without risking a rise in inflation, then an increase in investment must be matched by an increase in savings.

If government increases investment, the necessary savings will have to be provided by a cut in other spending or a rise in taxes. Should companies raise their capital spending there would have to be a compensating rise in savings. This could be generated by the corporate sector itself through a fall in the pay-out ratio (the proportion of post-tax profits paid out in dividends), an increased inflow of foreign savings, by households saving more, or by a fall in the fiscal deficit.

It is often claimed that companies do not need additional savings to pay for more investment because they are cash rich. But this does not affect the necessity for increased investment to be matched by increased savings, which are not provided by drawing down cash balances. These claims confuse 'stocks', such as cash on balance sheets, with 'flows' such as the level of corporate savings. The existence of large cash balances may reduce resistance to higher investment spending; but it does not reduce the need for more savings to finance it. Additional investment requires greater eagerness to invest as well as additional savings. High corporate cash balances should ease the former but will not provide the latter.

Figure 60 for the UK and Figure 61 for the US show that cash type assets are high by post-1987 standards. The earlier data for the US are not comparable because in the immediate post-war period there were limits on the rate of interest that banks were allowed to charge customers. The banks circumvented these by insisting that companies kept a proportion of their borrowings on deposit; these compensating balances artificially increased the cash element in corporate balance sheets.

US non-financial companies' leverage is near peak levels by historic standards, as I showed in Figure 25, whether this is measured gross or net of cash-type assets. Allowing for the distortion that compensating balances caused in

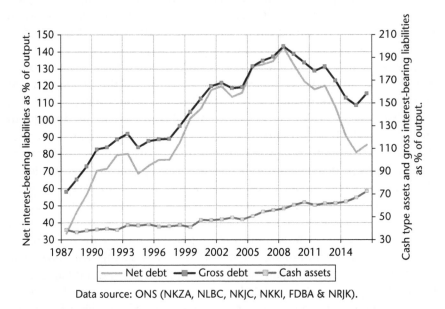

Data source: ONS (NKZA, NLBC, NKJC, NKKI, FDBA & NRJK).

Figure 60. UK: Private non-financial companies' gross and net debt

Data sources: Z1 Table B.103. & NIPA Table 1.14.

Figure 61. US: Non-financial corporate cash

the 1950s and 1960s, corporate cash balances are high in the US, but they have not prevented debt ratios rising since the end of 2009. UK data are not available before 1987, but are more encouraging in that leverage has continued to fall since 2008. Nonetheless Figure 60 shows that UK leverage is high, even by the standards of the limited historic data that we have. While high cash balances could ease decisions to increase investment, the high levels of debt, whether measured gross or net, makes a further rise in leverage a cause for concern.

The savings needed to finance increased business investment will not readily come from lower dividend pay-out ratios, as companies are loath to cut dividends. A reduction in buy-backs is therefore likely to be preferred. This will not raise corporate savings but is quite likely to raise savings in the household sector via the impact on the stock market.

As Figure 62 shows, companies have been the predominant net buyers of US equities for the past thirty years or so, reversing the previous pattern in which new issues exceeded reductions in equity capital through buy-backs and acquisitions. I showed in Figure 48 that companies have been net purchasers of equity in every quarter of the past eight years, with the exceptions of Q2 and Q3 of 2008, and have been the only consistent net buyer since then.

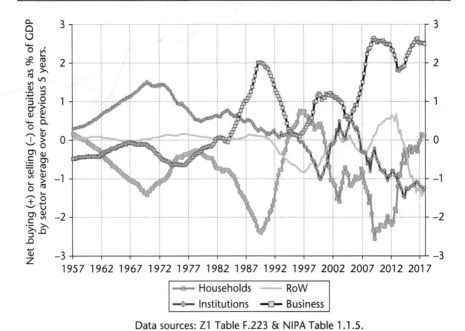

Data sources: Z1 Table F.223 & NIPA Table 1.1.5.

Figure 62. US: Long-term US net buyers of equities

The importance of corporate buying for the stock market is illustrated in Figure 63, which shows that corporate buying rises and falls with the level of the stock market.[1] Companies' net worth per share rises when buying is below net worth and falls when it is above. In the interests of shareholders, therefore, companies should buy shares when they are cheap rather than expensive; they don't because the opposite behaviour is in the interests of management.

A reduction in buy-backs does not show up as a change in corporate savings in the national accounts, as this method of distributing cash to shareholders is treated as a capital transfer rather than as an increase in shareholder incomes. Nonetheless a reduction in buy-backs is likely to result in a rise in private sector savings as a whole through the impact on household savings. As Figure 64 illustrates, these are low by historic standards, and as Figure 65 shows, a weak stock market has tended to push up the household savings' rate, particularly over the past forty years.[2]

As household savings rise and fall with the stock market, which is heavily influenced by the level of corporate buying, it is likely that if companies

---

[1] The positive correlation between corporate share purchases and the level of the S&P 500 over the past twenty years has an R^2 of 0.34.
[2] The R^2 coefficient for the positive correlation between personal savings and the stock market, both expressed relative to GDP, from Q1 1977 to Q4 2017 was 0.75.

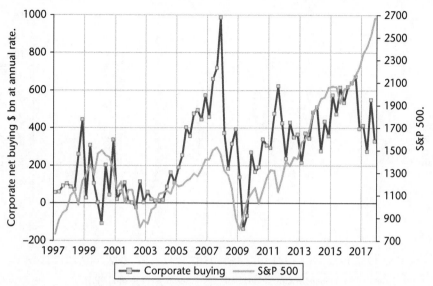

Data sources: Z1 Table F.223 and Standard & Poor's.

Figure 63. US: Corporate buying and the stock market

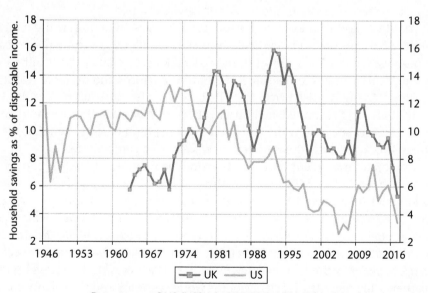

Data sources: ONS (NSSH & QWND) & NIPA Table 2.1.

Figure 64. UK and US: Household savings

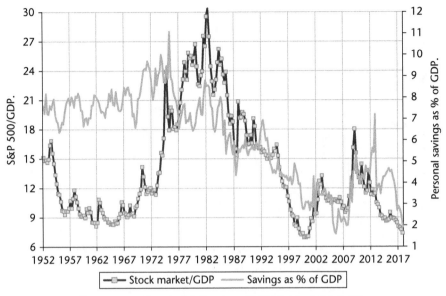

Data sources: Standard & Poor's and NIPA Tables 1.1.5 & 2.1.

Figure 65. US: Personal savings and the stock market

significantly reduce their net purchases of equity there will be a fall in the stock market and a rise in the household savings' rate.

Another reason for expecting a rise in US household savings is the under-funding of pension funds, particularly by states and local governments, whose unfunded liabilities are shown in the Federal Reserve's data as $1.9 trillion—though this assumes unrealistic levels of future returns and on more realistic assumptions is at least twice this.[3] If these deficits are reduced by a rise in contributions, the immediate impact will be to increase both household savings and fiscal deficits. If the reduction takes the form of lower benefits, then households may raise their discretionary savings to compensate.

Corporate investment may well therefore be financed at least in part by a rise in household savings, and in the absence of new trade barriers some additional help should be provided by a greater inflow of foreign savings. But this would show as a rise in the current account deficits, which, as Figure 66 illustrates, are already high and thus likely to exacerbate the already considerable trade frictions. It therefore seems unlikely that we can expect a large increase in the flow of foreign savings. The risk is that increased trade barriers will reduce the efficiency of the world economy and thus at any given level of demand will be inflationary.

[3] See Z1 Table L.120 as at 31 December 2017. In addition Z1 Table L.119 shows unfunded Federal liabilities of $2.0 trn.

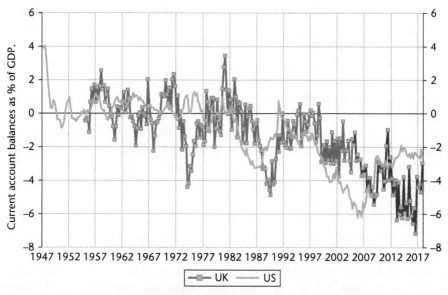

Data sources: ONS (HBOG & YBHA) and NIPA Tables 4.1 & 1.1.5.

Figure 66. UK and US: Current accounts

Even allowing for the change in the UK's relationship with the EU, the fall in sterling after Brexit is likely, if it persists, to lead to a reduction in the UK's current account deficit. The extent to which this will occur is widely disputed. It is generally agreed that the devaluation of 1992 was very success- ful in boosting net exports, but that the fall in 2008 and 2009 was less so. Bob Bischof, Chairman of the German-British Forum, Vice-President of the German-British Chamber of Industry and Commerce, and a member of the Official Monetary and Financial Institutions Forum (OMFIF) Advisory Board has argued that the perverse incentives of the bonus culture has been a major reason for the reduced impact of exchange rate changes on the UK's net exports.[4] This seems to me likely to be correct, judging from my own experi- ence. I was for many years Chairman of a UK manufacturing company which exported 80 per cent of its output. Declines in the exchange rate produced a large boost to profits, if we left our prices in foreign markets unchanged. We could simply pocket this benefit, or aim to increase future sales by reducing prices or raising our sales and marketing expenditure. The bonus culture will have increased the incentives to UK management to invest less of the profit boost in increasing exports than they would have done before. Investment in marketing is thus likely to be held back by the change in management

---

[4] Bischof (2016).

remuneration in a similar way to the negative impact on investment in equipment. The impact on the trade balance of a devaluation in sterling is thus likely to be less than it was in 1992.

But less is not nothing. The bonus culture will have little impact on unquoted companies or on companies owned by Japanese or by Continental Europeans. A likely result of a weaker sterling is the replacement of imported goods by those from UK sources, which are less likely to need additional marketing expenditure than would exports. The assumption that real devaluations do not reduce trade deficits is to deny the effectiveness of the price mechanism which has been working for at least the last 3,000 years.

The devaluation of sterling after Brexit is thus likely to improve the UK's international trade and current account balances but also unlikely to help finance a rise in corporate investment.

It seems unlikely that companies, households or foreigners will readily provide sufficient savings to finance a significant rise in corporate investment, and so a fall in the fiscal deficit seems likely to be needed. This fits with historic experience: fiscal deficits on both sides of the Atlantic have moved with the net borrowing of business, as shown for the UK in Figure 67 and for the US in Figure 68.

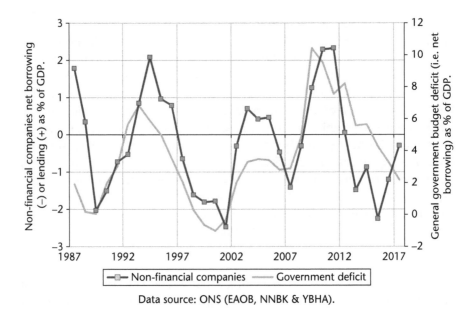

Data source: ONS (EAOB, NNBK & YBHA).

Figure 67. UK: Net borrowing and lending by non-financial companies and government

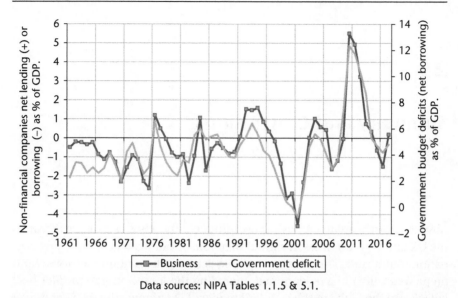

Data sources: NIPA Tables 1.1.5 & 5.1.

Figure 68. US: Net borrowing and lending by non-financial companies and government

Additional investment will boost demand, and as employment is so low either interest rates or taxes will have to rise if an increase in inflation is to be avoided. If investment rises, fiscal tightening is likely to make an essential and unpopular contribution to providing the necessary increase in savings.

25

Summary and Conclusions

Absent another financial crisis, poor productivity poses the major threat to the UK and US economies. It should therefore be our main economic preoccupation. But it isn't. The paucity of public debate reflects numerous follies and prejudices which I have identified, including the 'post hoc ergo propter hoc' fallacy and the faults in the standard model of economic growth. That model has distorted the debate by encouraging the belief that growth depends solely on the rate at which technology improves. I have shown that this is wrong, as we can have faster growth through encouraging rather than discouraging investment. This is fortunate as we have no way of speeding up the technological change.

In the past, if we avoided recessions or inflation then investment was strong enough to improve productivity at a satisfactory pace. Today in the UK and the US this no longer applies. We now have a supply not a demand problem. Many are reluctant to accept this. It has the horror of being a new idea and involves questioning traditional attitudes.

Economists, politicians and the media need to focus their attention on the problem of growth and to understand that it is not simply an issue of technology. The bonus culture threatens our future. It has depressed investment and stultified any improvement in productivity. Current policies provide no solutions, so we must introduce new policies that will increase investment and improve productivity. Without them we risk populist policies that will make our prospects worse.

I have made three suggestions; I hope they will be accepted:

  (i) to change the perverse incentives of modern management remuneration, or to change their impact on the economy;

 (ii) to require companies to publish their output and the working hours of their employees so that we can measure their productivity and compare it with earlier years and that of other companies;

(iii) to end the folly of allowing interest to be a deductible expense for corporation tax—a measure which would have the added advantage of reducing the risks of another financial crisis.

Changing either incentives or their impact is the most important of these, and I have suggested two different ways by which one or the other might be achieved. We may muddle through without these changes. I am not making a forecast that disaster would then be certain. I am, however, pointing out the threat that we face if recent trends are not an aberration—and it is surely rash to assume that they are. Bad outcomes are not certain, but when they are likely it is irresponsible to ignore policies by which we could avoid them.

It has been said that 'every truth passes through three stages before it is recognized. In the first it is ridiculed, in the second it is opposed, in the third it is regarded as self-evident'. The solving of problems and the search for truth requires new ideas, which also pass through stages. The first is silence, the second is debate, and the third is either rational acceptance or rejection.

The damage to the economy from the bonus culture is currently met with silence. The aim of this book is to get the issue debated, so that the idea will move to the self-evident category and be accompanied by the new policies we need.

Appendices

The Impact of Real and Nominal Interest Rates

The following is taken from Fair (2015), p. 456:

> Interest rates appear in the consumption and investment equations in the MC model for the US and other countries. Consumption and investment are in real terms, and a question is whether the interest rate in the equations should be nominal or real. This can be tested by adding both the nominal interest rate and a measure of expectations of future inflation to an equation and testing whether the coefficient estimate of the nominal interest rate is significantly negative and equal to the negative of the coefficient estimate of the expectations variable. If this is true, it is evidence in favor of the real interest rate. If instead the coefficient estimate of the nominal interest rate is significantly negative and the coefficient estimate of the expectations variable is insignificant, this is evidence in favor of the nominal interest rate. When the two variables are added for various measures of inflation expectations, the results are strongly in favor of the nominal interest rate. The coefficient estimate of the nominal interest rate is usually negative and significant, and the coefficient estimate of the inflation expectations variable is usually insignificant.

Measurement of the Net Capital Stock and Depreciation in the UK and the US

The approach of both the UK's Office of National Statistics (ONS) and the US's Bureau of Economic Analysis (BEA) are basically the same: the value of the capital stock and depreciation are estimated from historic investment and from survey data. The latter provide evidence for the value of second-hand equipment and thereby for the value of installed capital stock and for the rate at which capital depreciates. As these values will fall in line with the return that can be achieved by the purchaser they will reflect, inter alia, the expected profitability of the equipment, which will in turn reflect the rate of growth of real wages since the capital was installed. The use of survey data thus allows for the rate of growth of productivity when valuing the net capital stock and rates of capital consumption.

The ONS describes its approach as follows:

> Gross capital stocks tell us how much the economy's assets would cost to buy again as new, or their replacement cost. All of the fixed assets in the economy, that are still productive and in use, are added up to calculate this . . . This measure shows the value at the end of the year. This is mainly calculated as an intermediate step towards net capital stocks . . . Net capital stocks show the market value of fixed assets. The market value is the amount that the assets could be sold for, which will be lower than the value of gross capital stocks.[1]

The BEA uses both survey and historic data to measure the capital stock:

> There are two basic methods for measuring net stocks. The physical inventory method applies independently estimated prices to a direct count of the number of physical units of each type of asset. The perpetual inventory method cumulates past investment flows to indirectly estimate the value of the stock.[2]

The BEA bases its estimates of depreciation on survey data:

> BEA's estimates of depreciation are based on geometric depreciation patterns, which are supported by empirical studies of the prices of used equipment and structures in resale markets.[3]

---

[1] ONS (2014), p. 4.   [2] Bureau of Economic Analysis (2003), p. M–6.
[3] Bureau of Economic Analysis (2003), p. M–5.

The Gini Coefficient

The Office of National Statistics (ONS) publishes its estimate of the Gini Coefficient for the UK (see Figure 23). The method of calculation is described by the ONS as follows:

> The concept is expressed more formally by the Lorenz curve of household income distribution, from which the Gini coefficient can be calculated.
>
> Based on a ranking of households in order of ascending income, the Lorenz curve is a plot of the cumulative share of household income against the cumulative share of households. The curve will lie somewhere between two extremes.
>
> Complete equality, where income is shared equally among all households, results in a Lorenz curve represented by a straight line.
>
> The opposite extreme, complete inequality, where only 1 household has all the income and the rest have none, is represented by a Lorenz curve which comprises the horizontal axis and the right-hand vertical axis.
>
> The Gini coefficient is the area between the Lorenz curve of the income distribution and the diagonal line of complete equality, expressed as a proportion of the triangular area between the curves of complete equality and inequality.
>
> Complete equality would result in a Gini coefficient of zero, and complete inequality, a Gini coefficient of 100.
>
> All the Gini coefficients shown in the effects of taxes and benefits on household income are based on distributions of equivalised household income.
>
> Equivalisation is a standard methodology that takes into account the size and composition of households and adjusts their incomes to recognise differing demands on resources.

The Formulae for NTV

The capital stock is determined by the interaction of the level of NTV with the current level of technology. The latter is not a single point but a frontier. When NTV moves so as to allow the finance of more investment without any improvement in technology then $(\Delta K/K - \Delta L/L) > 0$. Thus improvements in technology will improve output without any increase in the volume of capital. Any difference in the growth rate of the volume of capital and the volume of labour will depend on changes in NTV which allow more capital to be financed without a change in technology. Changes in NTV can therefore be measured from the different growth rates of the volumes of capital and labour.

$$\text{So} \quad \Delta NTV = (\Delta K/K - \Delta L/L) \tag{1}$$

NTV can also be calculated independently from the changes in the constituents of NTV, which are profit margins, leverage, interest rates, the rate of corporation tax, and the hurdle rate on equity.

Changes in NTV are the aggregate result of changes in its constituents, which are:

1. the volume of capital (K);
2. profit margins, measured by profits after depreciation but before interest and corporation tax as a percentage of output measured after depreciation (M);
3. the amount of interest paid, calculated as the rate of interest (I) times the amount of debt (D);
4. leverage, which depends on the amount of equity (E) and capital (K);
5. the effective rate of Corporation Tax (T);
6. the hurdle rate on equity (H).

The interaction of NTV with the point on the technology frontier determines the amount of capital that will be financed. This in turn is determined by the level of RoE relative to the hurdle rate (H).

With output (Y) profits (Π) after depreciation but before interest and tax are

$$\Pi = Y \times M/100$$

Profits after depreciation and interest but before tax are

$$(Y \times M/100) - (I \times D)$$

where D is the proportion of K not financed by E, thus

$$D = K - E$$

So profits after depreciation and interest but before tax are

$$(Y \times M/100) - (I \times (K - E))$$

So profits after tax are

$$(Y \times M/100) - [(I \times (K - E))] \times [(100 - T) \div 100]$$

So RoE is

$$\{(Y \times M/100) - [(I \times (K - E))] \times [(100 - T) \div 100]\} \div E$$

$$\text{NTV changes if RoE} - H \neq 0$$

So

$$\Delta NTV = (\{(Y \times M/100) - [(I \times (K - E))] \times [(100 - T) \div 100]\} \div E) - H \qquad (2)$$

Because we have these two equations based on entirely different sources of data we can test the validity of the model. Because we do not have the all the data needed to solve Equation (2) we can only do this by showing, as I do, that the changes of the constituent parts of NTV are consistent with the changes in NTV derived from Equation (1).

US Profits as Published
Are Habitually Overstated

(i) We know this because the average earnings yield on US stocks from 1900 to 2013 was 7.37 per cent, which is higher than the total real return to investors over the same period of 6.15 per cent per annum.

(ii) The published pay-out ratios imply a more rapid rise in dividends per share than the observed change, as shown in Table A1 below. This could have been the result of overstated profits or through a fall in the pay-out ratio. I show that it must have been the result of the former by showing that the real growth of dividends would have been much slower than that implied by the profit data even if there had been no fall in the pay-out ratio.

Table A1. Comparison between implied and observed growth in US quoted company dividends

Average pay-out ratio 1900 to 2013 (A)	55.28%
Real returns to investors should equal average earnings yield (measured over the next 12 months) (B)	7.37%
Implied real growth of dividends (B) × (A) ÷100	3.3% per annum
Observed real growth of dividends	1.2% per annum
Actual pay-out ratio in 2013 was below average; had it been average growth of real dividends would have been	1.6% per annum

The Balassa–Samuelson Effect

Bela Balassa and Paul Samuelson in separate papers in 1964 put forward an explanation of why the Purchasing Power Parity (PPP) theory of exchange rates, even in the long run, would not hold if tradable goods and non-tradable goods are not perfect substitutes. Absolute PPP implies that the price of a basket of goods in one country converted at the nominal exchange rate should be the same as the price of a basket of goods in another country.

The Balassa–Samuelson theorem assumes two sectors: tradables and non-tradables. Consider two countries A, having a catch-up economy, and B, with a fully developed one. If P_A, P^T_A, and P^N_A are respectively the price level, price of tradable goods and price of non-tradable goods in country A, and P_B, P^T_B, and P^N_B similarly for country B, then

$$P_A = (P^T_A)^a \ (P^N_A)^{1-a}$$
$$P_B = (P^T_B)^b \ (P^N_B)^{1-b}$$

where a and b are the proportions of expenditure on tradables in countries A and B.[1] The price of tradables is determined by international arbitrage, therefore:

$$P^T_A = XP^T_B$$

where X is defined so that an increase in X corresponds to a depreciation for country A.

Domestic workers' wages are equalized by competition between the tradable and non-tradable sectors. Both sectors are assumed to have perfectly competitive product and labour markets so that the marginal product of labour equals the real wage. This implies that if the productivity of workers and capital in the sector producing traded goods grows faster than that of their counterparts in the sector producing non-traded goods (e.g. productivity in car plants grows faster than in barber shops), then the price of non-traded goods relative to traded goods should rise. Immobility of labour between countries prevents the equalization of international wage rates. Therefore:

$$MPL^T_A P^T_A = W^T_A = W_A = W^N_A = MPL^N_A P^N_A$$

---

[1] For simplicity, Cobb–Douglas demand functions are assumed so that the share of expenditure on tradables and non-tradables is constant.

$$MPL^T_B P^T_B = W^T_B = W_B = W^N_B = MPL^N_B P^N_B$$

where W^T_A = the wage of workers in country A in tradables and so on. This implies

$$P^N_A = MPL^T_A P^T_A \div MPL^N_A$$

If the share of tradables and non-tradables in expenditure is the same in each country then a = b. The equations can be arranged to demonstrate that the real exchange rate is:

$$1/x = P_A/XP_B = [(P^T_A)^a (P^N_A)^{1-a}] \div (XP^T_B)^a (XP^N_B)^{1-a}$$

$$= [MPL^T_A/MPL^N_A]^{1-a} \div [(MPL^T_B/MPL^N_B)^{1-a}]$$

where x = real exchange rate defined so that an increase corresponds to a real depreciation.

Both Balassa and Samuelson argued that technological progress is biased towards the production of tradables, and hence that as countries developed there would be a real appreciation in the exchange rate.

APPENDIX 7

Abolishing ACT Caused a Large Rise in the Effective Rate of Corporation Tax

I show in Figure A1 three different ways of calculating the rate of UK corporation tax since 1997. The figure also includes the changes promised by the former Chancellor of the Exchequer, George Osborne, for the financial years 2007 to 2020, which have been endorsed by the current government. The tax rate for private non-financial corporations (PNFCs), shown in Figure A1, is derived from the national accounts data and has been both highly volatile and persistently much higher than the rate of corporation tax to which companies appear to be liable. The volatility is probably due to the timing of quarterly payments and the high level is probably due, for the most part, to the

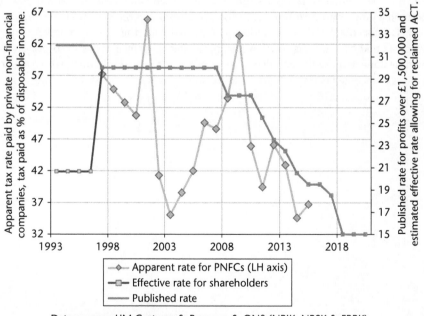

Data sources: HM Customs & Revenue & ONS (NRJK, NRSK & FBBK).

Figure A1. UK: Corporate tax rate

Table A2. Effective Corporation Tax with and without ACT as changed in 1997, with 60 per cent of profits paid out in dividends

	With ACT	Without ACT
Pre-tax profits (A)	100	100
Mainstream tax (B)	31	30
Profits after mainstream tax (C) = (A) − (B)	69	70
Cash dividend received by shareholders (D)	41.40	42
Tax reclaimed by shareholders (20% of gross dividend under ACT) (E)	10.35	0
Total cash receipts (F) = (D) + (E)	51.75	42
Retained profit (G) = (C) − (D)	27.60	28
Total increase in shareholders' wealth (H) = (F) + (G)	79.35	70
Effective tax rate (100- (H)) as % of (A)	20.65	30
Effective increase in tax rate	45%	

difference between the deduction in the national accounts for the consumption of capital, which allows for the impact of inflation, and the deduction for depreciation allowed for tax purposes in company accounts, which tends to be lower as it does not allow for the rise in the cost of new equipment due to inflation.

The difference between the 'published rate of corporation tax' and 'the effective rate for shareholders'[1] in Figure A1 arises from the abolition of ACT. I illustrate the effect of this change in Table A2. The calculations assume that 60 per cent of profits after tax are paid out in dividends and it should be noted that the extent to which tax increases with the change of system varies with this. The rate of corporation tax in the UK may therefore be defined as having risen in 1997 and then fallen back by 2015, or having been on a downward path since 2001. Press reports at the time of the change indicate that its impact was widely misunderstood. In particular the extent to which corporation tax had been increased was underappreciated and the emphasis was put on the damage done to those shareholders, such as pension funds and charities, which are not subject to income tax on their dividend income.

---

[1] The effective rate is that for shareholders, such as charities and pension funds, who are not liable to income tax.

Why Profit Margins in Mature Economies Are Expected to Revert to Their Mean

Economic theory supports the view that the labour and capital shares of output fluctuate around constant levels.

In general, theory suggests that the factor shares of output are determined by the nature of the production function, which explains how changes in labour and capital are translated into changes in output. The Cobb–Douglas production function, which assumes constant returns to scale and diminishing returns to factor accumulation, implies constant factor shares.

Production functions are used by economists to describe the relationship between inputs, such as labour L and capital K, and output Y. Consider the generic production function $Y = f(L,K)$. In explaining the evolution of the shares of output accounted for by L and K it is necessary to know how increases in L and K affect Y.

These increases are captured by the marginal product of L and K. Mathematically these are the first derivatives of the production function with respect to K and L, written as dY/dK and dY/dL.

In a competitive economy, capital will earn its marginal product (the rental rate r) and labour its marginal product (the wage rate w). This implies that

1. Labour's share of output $= wL/Y = ((dY/dL)L)/Y$ (1)
2. Capital's share of output $= rK/Y = ((dY/dK)K)/Y$ (2)

The shares of K and L in Y are therefore determined by the properties of the production function $Y = f(L,K)$ and the marginal products of labour and capital. While economists have considered many different specifications for f(L,K), the Cobb–Douglas production function is the most widely used.

The Cobb–Douglas production function takes the form $Y = AK^{(\alpha)}L^{(1-\alpha)}$, where Y is output, A is technology, K is the capital stock, L is labour and α is a parameter between zero and one which, as explained below, has a very specific interpretation.

The Cobb–Douglas production function exhibits two specific properties that are crucial in determining the factor shares. The first is constant returns to scale. This means that a doubling of inputs leads to a doubling of outputs. We can see this by multiplying K and L by a scalar m:

$$Y = A(mK)^{(\alpha)}(mL)^{(1-\alpha)} = m^{\alpha}m^{(1-\alpha)}Y = mY$$

Secondly, there is decreasing marginal productivity. This means that the derivatives of the marginal products are negative. Mathematically, the first derivative of the Cobb–Douglas production function with respect to K is

$$dY/dK = \alpha AK^{(\alpha-1)}L^{(1-\alpha)}$$

Differentiating again, we see that

$$d^2Y/dK^2 = \alpha(1-\alpha)AK^{(\alpha-2)}L^{(1-\alpha)} < 0.$$

This says that while an extra unit of capital increases output there are diminishing returns, with each extra addition to the capital stock generating a smaller increase in output than the preceding one. A similar argument holds for labour.

Substituting the expressions for dY/dK and dY/dL implied by the Cobb–Douglas production function in (1) and (2) we see that labour and capital have constant factor shares:

Labour's share of output $= wL/Y = (1-\alpha)AK^{\alpha}L^{-\alpha}L/Y = (1-\alpha)$

Capital's share of output $= rK/Y = \alpha AK^{(\alpha-1)}L^{(1-\alpha)}L/Y = \alpha$

Therefore α and $(1-\alpha)$ are the shares of labour and capital in output.

Published Data on Quoted US Non-financial Companies

As explained in the text data profit margins were average for the year to 31st March 2014, which means that the data in Tables A3 and A4 should not be distorted by cyclical factors.

Table A3. Data Comparisons: 400 non-financial companies in S&P 500 past 12 months as at 9 July 2014 (Data source: Standard & Poor's using companies' data)

	US $ bn.
Sales	9,197
Operating profit	1,192
Pre-tax profit	1,115
Net profit after tax	814
Depreciation and amortisation	465
Equity	4,788
Net debt	1,187
Net debt as % of equity	24.8%
Capital employed	5,975

Table A4. Resulting Ratios as at 29 August 2014

Market capitalization (as at 29 August 2014)	$16,355 bn
P/E	20.09
P/Cash flow	12.79
Tax rate	26.97
Price/Book	3.42
RoE	17.00
RoC	27.73

Glossary

Bonus culture The attitudes and behaviour resulting from the dramatic change in the amounts and bonus element of management remuneration in the decade from 1990 to 2000.

Bonus element The proportion of total remuneration not dependent on a fixed salary.

Buy-backs The reduction of the equity capital of companies through share purchases.

Capital consumption The loss in the value of plant and equipment arising from depreciation (see below) and from changes in non-technology variables NTV (see below).

Capital consumption adjustment (CC) Company profits habitually use historic cost for calculating depreciation. But in real terms depreciation will be affected by inflation and this adjustment seeks to remove the resulting distortion from the national accounts.

Capital stock value (capital value) The second-hand value of plant and equipment as shown in surveys by the ONS for the UK and the BEA for the US.

Capital stock volume (capital volume) The original cost, measured at constant prices, of all plant and equipment that has not been scrapped.

Capital/output ratio The ratio of the capital stock (either value or volume) to output, both measured at current prices.

Cobb-Douglas Production Function Shows that, with constant returns to scale, the labour and profit shares of output are stable when profits are measured net of capital consumption.

Coefficient of determination R^2 A measure used to assess the strength of any underlying relationship between two variables. It is the square of the correlation coefficient (see below).

Consensus interpretation / standard interpretation My term for the ways in which Total Factor Productivity has usually and in my view wrongly been measured.

Corporate veil The barrier which allows and causes companies to behave other than if they were directly operated by their shareholders, who are assumed for the purpose to have identical aims and wishes.

Correlation coefficient A measure used to assess the strength of any underlying relationship between two variables. It is the square root of the coefficient of determination R^2 (see above).

Cost of equity The return needed on new investment to match the cost of adding to a company's equity. In the US it appears to have been mean-reverting in the long run at around 6% p.a. in real terms.

Cyclically adjusted PE (CAPE) One of two valid measures of the value of the US equity market (see *q ratio* below for the other). Measured at constant prices it is the ratio of the share price to the mean earnings per share (EPS) of the S&P 500 over the past 10 years. Its validity depends on the mean reversion of the real return on equities and the assumption that the overstatement of US profits in published accounts is stable over time.

Data mining The process of manipulating a set of data in an attempt to prove a hypothesis.

Demographic deficit (−) /**surplus** (+) The annual growth rate of the number of people of working age (usually defined as between 15 and 65) minus the annual growth rate of the total population.

Depreciation The loss over time in the value of plant and equipment, mainly through the rise in real wages and the consequent fall in profit margins; often misrepresented as the cost of maintenance.

Dividend yield The dividend per share divided by the share price, expressed as a percentage.

Earnings per share (EPS) Net profit after tax divided by the number of shares outstanding.

Earnings' yield The EPS × 100 divided by the share price. It is therefore equivalent to 100/PE (see below) ; for example, a PE of 20 is the same as an earnings' yield of 5%.

Efficient Markets Hypothesis (EMH) States that every security's price equals its investment value at all times.

Endogenous Having an internal cause or origin.

Exogenous Having an external cause or origin.

Fair value The price that a security, or the stock market in aggregate, would have if it were correctly valued. It follows that price and fair value would always be the same if the EMH held.

Final output The value of the output of the economy or a company after deducting intermediate output (see below) to avoid double counting. It differs from sales, which includes intermediate output.

Fiscal deficit (−) /**surplus** (+) Government income minus government spending.

Full employment The level of unemployment consistent with a stable level of inflation.

GINI Coefficient The most widely used measure of the income inequality.

Hours worked The total number of hours worked by those employed.

Hurdle rate The minimum return on equity required to justify new investment.

Intangible assets (intangibles) These are the assets of companies which are neither financial, such as cash on deposit, nor physical, such as plant and equipment. They are typically represented by brand names and patents but can cover many other things.

Intellectual property (IP) The assumed value of intangibles.

Intermediate output The value of goods and services which are used to produce final output and whose value must be deducted to avoid double counting of output.

Inventory adjustment (IVA) A rise in the current prices of inventories will affect profits based on the historic cost convention; no profit in real terms has been made and this adjustment is used in the national accounts to try to allow for this difference.

Labour productivity (productivity) Output, measured either before or after capital consumption, divided by numbers employed or hours worked.

Leverage (gearing) The proportion of capital employed that is provided by debt rather than equity. Alternative measures are the ratio of debt, gross or net, to output.

Linear Exhibiting directly proportional changes in two related quantities which can thus be represented on a graph by a straight line.

Log numbers In some of the charts I use log numbers. This is usually done to allow the eye to recognise that the swings in the chart around their average value are such that the size of falls below average is balanced by those above. Using percentage changes for example, gives a distorted picture because a fall of 50% requires a rise of 100% to restore the original value.

Maintenance The cost of maintaining equipment so that its productive capacity is undamaged.

Mean Either the arithmetic mean, which is sum of the values of n numbers in a series divided by n, or the geometric mean, which is the nth root of their product.

Mean reversion Some series (examples are the ratio of capital value to net domestic product, q and CAPE) have a tendency to move back to around their average. This is statistically measured by the Augmented Dickie-Fuller Test. If sufficient data are available when measured in logs, the arithmetic mean will be the same as the linear trend and I illustrate this in some of the charts.

Median For a set of values, the number for which there are as many of higher value as of lower.

Model A simplification of a complex system made to help understand it and test its properties.

National accounts The data for the combined income, output and expenditure of a nation, together with the more detailed data used in their compilation and associated series.

Negative serial correlation The behaviour of a series, such as the real return on equities, in which above-average past returns indicate the probability of below-average future returns and vice versa.

Net worth The net value of a company after deducting its financial liabilities. Net worth is therefore the same as corporate equity. It may be shown at book value or after adjustment to allow for price changes.

Nominal returns Returns defined in terms of current prices.

Non-accelerating inflationary rate of unemployment (NAIRU) The minimum level of unemployment consistent with a stable rate of unemployment in conditions of stable inflationary expectations.

Non-financial companies and non-financial corporate sector The corporate sector is divided into non-financial and financial companies. The dividing line is fairly obvious with banking, insurance and financial advice being distinguished from manufacturing and non-financial services. Where manufacturing companies have financial subsidiaries their activities are split in the national accounts between the two sectors.

Non-technology variables (NTV) In my TFP model the amount of current technology in which it is worth investing is determined by leverage, interest rates, corporation tax, profit margins and the equity hurdle rate, which constitute NTV in aggregate.

Participation rate The rate of those employed plus those seeking work as a percentage of those of working age.

PE (PE multiple or P/E) The price per share divided by the earnings per share, therefore also the market value of a company, or of the stock market in aggregate, divided by profits after tax.

Post hoc fallacy My compressed version of the logical fallacy that something which follows something else has been caused by it.

Private sector The economy is divided into four main sectors; households, corporations, government and foreigners. The first two together comprise the private sector.

Profit margins The ratio of profit, measured in various ways, to output or sales.

Public sector The government sector of the economy.

q ratio Comes in two forms Tobin's q and equity q. The former is the ratio of market value to debt of the corporate sector, usually limited because of data problems to the non-financial sector. Equity q, the form used in this book, is the market value of the non-financial corporate sector divided by its net worth at replacement cost, expressed as a ratio to its long-term average.

Quantitative easing (QE) The purchase by a central bank of bonds financed by deposits that commercial banks have with it. Effectively a way of shortening the duration of government debt.

Quoted (listed) companies Companies quoted on stock markets.

Random Walk Hypothesis This is the restricted version of the EMH which assumes that the variations from long-term averages in future returns are independent of past returns. Shown to be false by the variance compression (see below) of equity returns.

Real returns Returns adjusted for inflation.

Research and Development (R&D) Costs incurred in finding new or improved products or more efficient ways to produce existing ones.

Return on Equity (RoE) Profits after tax as a percentage of net worth.

Scrapping Ceasing to employ equipment.

Standard deviation This measures the variability of distributions, for example of returns. It is the square root of the variance (see below).

Tangible assets In contrast to intangibles these are the physical assets of companies, such as plant and equipment.

Total Factor Productivity (TFP) The contribution to growth that does not come from increases in the volumes of labour and capital.

Variance A measure of the variability of distributions, calculated as the average of the squares of the difference between the observed returns and their mean.

Variance compression This occurs when variance falls over time by more than it would if returns were random.

Volatility This is measured by the standard deviation or the variance.

Working age population The number of people aged 15 to 65.

Write-offs Reductions in the book values of assets.

Bibliography

Asker, John, Joan Farre-Mensa and Alexander Ljungqvist (2015), 'Corporate Investment and Stock Market Listing: A Puzzle?' *Review of Financial Studies* 28(2): 342–90.

Bénabou, Roland and Jean Tirole (2016), 'Bonus Culture: Competitive Pay, Screening, and Multitasking', *Journal of Political Economy* 124(2): 305–70.

Bernanke, Ben (2004), 'The Great Moderation', speech to the Eastern Economic Association, 20 February 2004.

Bishof, Bob (2016), 'Tackling the UK's export malaise: Limits to Anglo-Saxon Corporate Governance Model', OMFIF, 15 September 2016.

Borio Claudio, Leonardo Gambacorta and Boris Hofmann (2015), 'The influence of monetary policy on bank profitability', Bank for International Settlements, BIS Working Paper 514.

Breedon, Francis (1995), 'Bond prices and market expectations of inflation'. *Bank of England Quarterly Bulletin* (May): 160–5.

Bureau of Economic Analysis (2003), *Fixed Assets and Consumer Durable Goods in the United States, 1925–99* (Washington, DC: U.S. Government Printing Office).

Byrne, David M., John G. Fernald and Marshall B. Reinsdorf (2016), 'Does the United States have a productivity slowdown or a measurement problem?', *Brookings Papers on Economic Activity* (Spring 2016): 109–82.

Corrado, Carol, Charles Hulten and Daniel Sichel (2009), 'Intangible Capital and Economic Growth', *Review of Income and Wealth* 55(3): 661–85.

Deutsch, David and Artur Ekert (2012), 'Beyond the Quantum Horizon', *Scientific American* 307(3) (September): 84–9.

Donaldson, John B., Natalia Gershun and Marc P. Giannoni (2011), 'Some Unpleasant General Equilibrium Implications of Executive Incentive Compensation Contracts'. Federal Reserve Bank of New York Staff Report no. 531 (December 2011).

Donnan, Shawn (2016), 'Inequality decreased after global financial crisis', *Financial Times*, 2 October 2016.

Döttling, Robert, Germán Gutiérrez and Thomas Philippon (2017), 'Is there an investment gap in advanced economies? If so why?', in *Investment and growth in advanced economies: Conference Proceedings*, ECB Forum on Central Banking, 26–28 June 2017, Sintra, Portugal, pp. 129–93.

Dunkley, Emma (2015), 'UK banks need to work harder on profitability, study finds', *Financial Times*, 7 April 2015.

Fair Ray C. (2015), 'Reflections on macroeconometric modelling', *B.E. Journal of Macroeconomics* 15(1): 445–66.

Feinstein, C. H. (1976), *Statistical Tables of National Income, Expenditure and Output of the UK, 1855–1965* (Cambridge: Cambridge University Press).

Galbraith, John Kenneth (1955), *The Great Crash, 1929* (Boston, MA: Houghton Mifflin).

Ghosh, Swarti R. and Aart Kraay (2000), 'Measuring growth in total factor productivity', World Bank PREM Notes No. 42.

Giles, Chris (2018), 'UK's biggest companies are productivity slackers', *Financial Times*, 24 May 2018.

Gordon, Robert J. (2016), *The Rise and Fall of American Growth: The U.S. Standard of Living since the Civil War* (Princeton, NJ: Princeton University Press).

Hall, Robert E. and Dale W. Jorgensen (1967), 'Tax Policy and Investment Behavior', *American Economic Review* 57(3): 391–414.

Hulten Charles R. (2001), 'Total Factor Productivity: A Short Biography', in Charles R. Hulten, Edwin R. Dean and Michael J. Harper (eds), *New Developments in Productivity Analysis* (Chicago: University of Chcago Press), pp. 1–54.

King, Mervyn (2016), *The End of Alchemy: Money Banking and the Future of the Global Economy* (London: Little, Brown, 2016).

Krugman, Paul (2016), 'Robber Baron Recessions', *New York Times*, 18 April 2016.

Maddison, Angus (2003), *The World Economy: Historical Statistics* (Paris: OECD Publishing).

Mirrlees, James, Stuart Adam, Tim Besley, Richard Blundell, Stephen Bond, Robert Chote, Malcolm Gammie, Paul Johnson, Gareth Myles and James M. Poterba (2011), *Tax by Design: The Mirrlees Review* (Oxford: Oxford University Press).

Mokyr, Joel (2016), *A Culture of Growth: The Origins of the Modern Economy* (Princeton, NJ: Princeton University Press).

Noonan, Laura (2016), 'Investment banks' hopes of big savings a "pipe dream"', *Financial Times*, 2 June 2016.

OECD (2009), *Measuring Capital: OECD Manual 2009*, 2nd edn (Paris: OECD Publishing).

ONS (2014), 'Capital Costs and Fixed Capital Consumption, UK: 2014', Office for National Statistics, 14 November 2014.

Popper, Karl (1959), *The Logic of Scientific Discovery* (London: Hutchinson).

Pradhan, Manoj, Charles Goodhart and Patryk Drozdzik (2016), *Life after Debt* (New York: Morgan Stanley).

Reinhart, Carmen M. and Kenneth S. Rogoff (2009), *This Time is Different: Eight Centuries of Financial Folly* (Princeton, NJ: Princeton University Press).

Riley, Rebecca, Ana Rincon-Aznar and Lea Samek (2018), 'Below the Aggregate: A Sectoral Account of the UK Productivity Puzzle', ESCoE Discussion Paper 2018-06, Economic Statistics Centre of Excellence in collaboration with Office for National Statistics.

Shackelton, Robert (2018), 'Estimating and Projecting Potential Output Using CBO's Forecasting Growth Model', Congressional Budget Office Working Paper 2018-03 (February).

Shiller, Robert (2000), *Irrational Exuberance* (Princeton, NJ: Princeton University Press).

Smithers, Andrew (2009), Wall Street Revalued: Imperfect Markets and Inept Central Bankers (Chichester: Wiley).

Smithers, Andrew (2016), 'How Managerial Incentives Affect Economic Performance', *World Economics* 17(1).

Smithers, Andrew (2017), 'Building a New Testable Model to Estimate Total Factor Productivity', *World Economics* 18(2).

Smithers, Andrew, and Stephen Wright (2000), *Valuing Wall Street: Protecting wealth in turbulent markets* (New York: McGraw-Hill).

Smithers, Andrew, and Stephen Wright (2002), 'Stock Markets and Central Bankers: The Economic Consequences of Alan Greenspan', *World Economics* 3(1).

Snowdon, Brian (2001), 'Keeping the Keynesian Faith: Alan Blinder on the evolution of macroeconomics', *World Economics* 2(2).

Solow, Robert M. (1956), 'A Contribution to the Theory of Economic Growth', *Quarterly Journal of Economics* 70(1): 65–94.

Solow, R. M., J. Tobin, C. C. von Weizsacker and M. Yaari, 'Neoclassical Growth with Fixed Factor Proportions', *Review of Economic Studies* 33(2): 79–115.

Taylor, Martin (2016), 'Banking in the tundra', speech to the Official Monetary and Financial Institutions Forum, 25 May 2016.

Tett, Gillian (2017), 'Donald Trump has to make start-up America great again', *Financial Times*, 19 January 2017.

Vernon, J. R. (1994), 'Unemployment Ratios in Postbellum America: 1869–1899', *Journal of Macroeconomics* 16(4): 701–14.

White, William R. (2015), 'The Ultra-Easy Money Experiment', 5th Lectio Minghetti, Bruno Leoni Institute, Rome, 20 October 2015.

Index

Note: (f) following a locator indicates a Figure; "n" following a locator indicates a Footnote; (t) following a locator indicates a Table.